BE A WRITING MACHINE

Write Faster and Smarter, Beat Writer's Block, and
Be Prolific

M.L. RONN

Contents

Writer's Block Part 1: How to Beat It Every Time

Writer's Block Part 2: General Maintenance Strategies to Keep You Motivated

Writer's Block Part 3: Strategies to Combat Lack of Inspiration

Writer's Block Part 4: Strategies to Combat Fear

What You'll Learn from This Book

Let's skip the fluffy stuff for a minute and talk about the two simple things you're going to learn in this book.

First, you're going to learn how to write books faster. Way faster. This will be easy.

Second, you're going to learn how to write smarter. This will be hard. Crazy hard. But you will be better for it.

When you're done with this book, you'll have a step-by-step roadmap on how to become the prolific writer you've always wanted to be.

You'll be a writing machine.

What if you could develop a consistent daily writing habit and finish a new novel every few weeks? Every few *days*? What would that mean for your writing career?

We all know that writing more books means more readers and therefore more money. But for many of us, just writing the next chapter is a struggle.

Writing isn't easy. If it was, then everyone would be prolific.

There are tricks to make the words flow easier. Fortunately, it doesn't involve any extra intelligence or wisdom.

I have used the strategies in this book to write 6-8 books on average every year since 2014. I have written dozens of novels in the same amount of time it takes many authors to write a few. My novels range from 40,000 to 70,000 words. The techniques in this book will help you with any fiction genre.

You're going to learn a simple system that you can adapt to suit your own lifestyle and career goals. It doesn't matter whether you're a part-time or a full-time author. All you need is an open mind and a willingness to try something new.

A Little about Me

Here's my story and why I'm qualified to write this book.

In July 2012, my wife rushed me to the emergency room. I was experiencing horrible stomach cramps, so bad I couldn't even see straight. Little did I know that the restaurant I'd visited the night before had served me tainted food, resulting in the worst food poisoning of my life.

I'll spare you the details of my hospital visit, but while I was there, I caught an infection.

I spent an entire month doped up on morphine, staring at a wall. I had a lot of time to think about my life.

Until then, I had been a sometime writer. I wrote whenever the muse moved me. I wasn't serious about it.

Something on that hospital bed made me change my mind.

I had a spiritual awakening. Among my many hallucinations, I visualized myself as a published author. It made me so happy—I felt an incredible euphoria just thinking about it. (Okay, the euphoria probably came from the morphine, but hey, details…)

I swore right then and there on that hospital bed that I would become a serious writer, no matter what.

Fortunately, I beat the infection and escaped from the

hospital. The very week I came home, an article came out on the front page of *USA Today* about the particular strain of bacteria that I had, and how it was killing an alarming amount of people all over the United States.

Basically, I could have died.

That was life-changing for me.

The next week, I remember sitting down at my kitchen table and trying to write a short story. I didn't know how to start it, and I stared at a blank screen for hours.

I remember an intense wave of fear. My inner critic kicked in.

"You'll never be able to write," it said. "This story will fail. Give up now before you embarrass yourself."

I remember thinking, "Why am I scared? I just spent a month in the hospital on my deathbed and wasn't scared of dying, so why the hell am I scared about writing this short story?"

Something clicked.

Then I stopped being afraid of just about everything in my life.

Compared to what I had been through, "fear," in the writer's sense of the word, stopped scaring me. I learned how to fight my fear every time it tried to stop me.

And then, one morning, four years later, I woke up and realized I had written over 40 books, with no signs of slowing down.

I wrote those books while becoming a father for the first time.

I wrote those books while climbing the corporate ladder at a Fortune 100 insurance company in the United States, with management-level responsibility.

I wrote those books while attending law school in the evenings.

I wrote those books while being a friend, father, son,

husband, and all the thousand other things my loved ones needed me to be.

I wrote those books while hosting a podcast, running a YouTube channel, mentoring other authors, and finding ways to give back to the indie author community as a liaison for the Alliance of Independent Authors.

If anyone should have a thousand excuses not to write, it should be me. If you look at my life, it's a miracle that I can even *think* about writing.

But that's enough about my credentials. I just wanted to get those out of the way to show you that I know the topic of writing fast and smart. And I know it well.

If I can do this, it's only right for me to share some of my secrets so that you can do it too.

Quick Overview of This Book's Structure

- The **Mindset** chapter will teach you how you need to adapt your mindset in order to reach new levels of productivity. I can't promise I won't go hippie on you, but I can promise that you'll get a fresh perspective that you haven't seen before.
- The **Tools** chapter will show you what tools I use to hit crazy word counts every day.
- The **Time Management** chapter will teach you how to organize your limited time and make the most of it.
- The **Write Smart** chapter teaches you how to be smart about your novel writing. It will give you a prolific author's perspective on what you can do to produce high numbers of books year after year.
- The **Writer's Block** chapter is the most important in the book. I will show you the root causes of

writer's block and my strategies on beating it every time. The latter part of this section is organized into quick hit strategies that you can refer to whenever you find yourself in a rough patch in your work in progress.

My goal for you is to pull back the curtain on how I do it and give you a different perspective on writing fast.

Remember, prolific isn't just about writing one book fast. It's about producing book after book after book, rain or shine, no matter what. It's about learning how to be systematic.

Proficient fiction writers will benefit the most from this book. If you've been through the novel writing process a few times, then the strategies in this book will make more sense to you. If you don't write fiction, you can still use the strategies here, but know that your mileage may vary.

If you're in this for the long haul and are ready to take your word counts to new, consistent heights, then read on.

Mindset: You Cannot Be Prolific Without Getting Your Mind Correct

The first step to writing fast and developing a prolific career is developing the right mindset.

I know, I know, you're probably thinking that you've heard all the typical mindset crap before.

I'm not talking about that.

I don't care whether you state spiritual affirmations to yourself in the shower, meditate, or have a daily ritual.

Seriously. You do whatever you think you have to do to get into the right mindset. I can't teach you that.

But I can give you some useful things to consider.

You Cannot Be Prolific Without the Right Mindset

Most authors I know just write without thinking too much about their mental state. They're mostly concerned about money or marketing.

But think about this: what happens if you wake up one

morning three years from now and wonder why you're doing all of this in the first place? How will you handle that?

Have you really *thought* about it?

Most people don't.

They don't think far enough ahead to realize that one day they will burn out.

Everyone burns out.

If you're going to be a writing machine, you're going to be producing high numbers of novels over time.

In order to sustain that volume over time, you have to be in the right mindset.

You have to know how to fill your spiritual well. That's how you can learn to minimize your burn out and get through it unscathed.

Otherwise, you may have a few good years here and there, but you'll risk undoing all your success.

The best way to prevent long-term burnout is to find out what motivates you.

A Personal Example

Some people have asked me why I am writing this book. In a way, I'm pulling back the curtains and exposing my business and work practices.

Let me tell you why I am okay with that.

In 2012, when I had my spiritual awakening, I knew that being a writer was the only thing I could ever see myself doing long-term.

The more I published, the more I realized that my decision to become a writer was the right one.

When I was a baby, my father and mother divorced.

I only ever met my father once, and that was for half an

hour. He didn't want anything to do with me. I never knew why.

Throughout my whole life, I carried a lot of pain and feelings of abandonment. When I hit my thirties and had a family of my own, I decided to reach out to him again to see if I could reconcile with him. It was important for me emotionally and physically.

I found him on Facebook. And I reached out.

He ignored me.

How do I know that?

Because Facebook doesn't lie, that's why.

I really struggled with that. It hurt me.

Anyway, I don't want to bore you with my life story.

I tell you this because my father's second rejection of me shook me so deeply that I wasn't prepared for it.

I thought about my life and everything I had achieved up to that point. I turned to God and spirituality, and to be completely honest with you, I couldn't find anything there that could help me.

The only thing I could turn to was my writing.

And then I realized: writing for me *is* my spirituality. It's how I deal with my problems and face the world.

The act of writing itself is as sacred as prayer for me.

When I am in the middle of a book, improvising and coming up with new and random ideas, I am in my element. I'm writing, but I'm not really writing; something is writing through me and I am just the instrument (probably why I never remember what happens in my stories…).

That's special. And it's not a coincidence.

Writing is how I connect with God. It's the only way I have been able to channel my energy and understand my life and the world and people around me.

Nothing taught me that more forcefully than the interactions with my father.

So, for me, writing is the way for me to express myself and wrestle with emotions and feelings that maybe readers themselves feel.

If I'm honest, writing is about coping with the difficulties in my life.

If I'm really honest, writing is about becoming the best possible version of myself in spite of my life's difficulties (being abandoned by my father, being raised by a single mother, being a black man in the United States, being "different" in general). That doesn't just apply to me—it applies to my characters, too. This theme shows up in my work over and over. Not surprisingly, some of my heroes have abandonment issues, too.

If I'm really, really honest, writing is the only thing that keeps me functional.

Books keep avid readers functional, too. Books help them see the world in a new way. Books help them cope with all the bullshit that goes on in their lives, too.

So, my vision aligns with my readers'.

Books help people. They help us expand our minds and be better people.

So I know that when I'm writing, I'm helping others, too.

I'm helping that guy who comes home from work every day and likes to escape into a good book.

I'm helping the woman who reads for adventure and thrill.

And that, in and of itself, is enough for me.

I am prolific because I have connected completely with the reason I was put on this Earth. I'm prolific because the experiences in my life have allowed me to remove all fear and therefore work harder and faster than I ever thought possible. I fear nothing and no one. I give zero fucks about what people think about me or my work; I just sit down and I make stuff up, trusting that my work is making a difference in people's lives.

Nothing fills my spiritual and creative well like writing.

Thinking about the next story is what gets me out of bed in the morning every day.

Not marketing.

Not money.

Not being famous.

Just doing the work is enough for me.

How About You?

Many writers say that writing motivates them, but...

When their sales drop, they become discouraged.

When someone gives them a bad review, they sulk over it.

When Amazon or Apple or some other big retailer changes their algorithms and affects the writer's success, they start thinking whether they really want to do this.

So, the answer for those people is *no*, writing does not (necessarily) fill their spiritual wells.

If you want to be a writer for a very long time, the answer for you has to be an unequivocal, unshakeable, indisputable *yes*.

No "yes, buts."

But yes. Make that a cosmic, orgasmic yes, actually.

Bad things will happen to you in your writing career more often than good things. At least when you're starting out. You have to have the mental mindset to deal with the setbacks.

If writing in and of itself is not your sole motivator, I would ask you to have a serious conversation with yourself on why it's not.

Connect with your purpose. We all have one. For you, I suspect that it's writing. Find out why.

Keep that spiritual well full.

When you do, nothing will be able to stop you.

· · ·

Eliminate All Expectations and Stop Comparing Yourself to Other Authors (Seriously)

One of my favorite movie lines is in *Training Day* when Denzel Washington says, "The shit's chess, it ain't checkers."

When we first start as authors, everything seems so simple. Write your book, throw it up on Amazon, and sit back and laugh as the money pours in.

Not.

So much unhappiness comes from those unrealistic expectations as we slowly realize that the book business is more complicated and nuanced than we thought. It takes a lot of strategy, intention, hard work, and luck.

Publishing is a lot of things, but it's not easy.

It's chess, not checkers. And chess is a tough game, especially when you're playing against many masters with higher skill levels than you.

Do yourself a favor and throw all your expectations out the window.

If you expect success and success doesn't happen because your expectations aren't realistic, there goes your mindset. That kind of damage takes a lot of time to repair.

I stopped making expectations around my second year of publishing. I have no expectations about any book I write. I've written books that I've spent months and months on, only for them to do poorly at launch. I've written some books in record time, published them without thinking about them, only to find that they sell. Most of my books lie somewhere in between.

Why should you avoid expectations?

Because as an author, it's impossible for you to have a picture of "good."

You cannot truly set accurate expectations for your career that aren't counterproductive in some way.

How should your next series be performing? That's a deceptive question because it invites comparison to others. Comparing yourself to other people is one of the most dangerous, destructive things you can do in this business.

Just because Author A's space fantasy series made him a bestseller doesn't mean that your space fantasy series will do the same for you, even if you use the same cover designer, similar characters, and have a similar story. I've fallen into that trap many times.

Again, back to the picture of "good."

There is no picture, no north star, no benchmark that you can use to set expectations for yourself and your career. The only information you can use is your own experience.

Now, keep in mind that I'm telling you to avoid setting expectations.

I'm *not* telling you to avoid setting goals.

I'm not telling you to avoid setting milestones.

I'm not telling you to avoid planning.

All I'm saying is to use the only reliable benchmark you have: your own experience. It will grow over time, giving you more data to make decisions from.

If you set any expectations for yourself, use these:

1. You will write every day.
2. You will not compare yourself to others.
3. You will improve your writing and marketing with every new book.
4. You will have fun with your writing.

Those are much healthier expectations, and the foundation for a long, prolific career.

.   .   .

Be Attached and Unattached to Your Work…at the Same Time

When I was early in my writing career, I stumbled upon a weird little philosophy book that changed my outlook on writing: *The Complete Works of Swami Vivekananda.*

Swami Vivekananda was a Hindu monk who introduced the western world to Hindu teachings. He lived an incredible life, and as I read his teachings, they spoke to me.

Swami Vivekananda wrote some epic stuff. Check out these quotes and think about them in the perspective of a writer:

> "…a man ought to live in this world like a lotus leaf, grows in water but is never moistened by water; so a man ought to live in the world—his heart to God and his hands to work."

> "To the Hindu, man is not traveling from error to truth, but from truth to truth, from lower to higher truth."

> "Man is, as it were, a centre, and is attracting all the powers of the universe towards himself, and in this centre is fusing them all and again sending them off in a big current."

> "You must remember that all work is simply to bring out the power of the mind which is already there, to wake up the soul."

And my favorite:

"We must do the work and find out the motive power that prompts us; and, almost without exception, in the first years, we shall find that our motives are always selfish; but gradually this self-ishness will melt by persistence, till at last will come the time when we shall be able to do really unselfish work."

I have no idea how I found his book, but I was glad that I did, and I stayed up all night for days reading it.

Swami Vivekananda was a deep thinker, and his writing has an uncanny, psychic quality to it, almost as if he's speaking directly to you and through you at the same time.

Aside from expanding my mind to Hindu philosophy, he taught me an early important lesson that informs how I think about my work.

Here's another quote, and it's a long one, but please read it (or if you must, skip to a summary below).

"At the same time, we not only want this mighty power of love, this mighty power of attachment, the power of throwing our whole soul upon a single object, losing ourselves and letting ourselves be annihilated...but we want to be higher even than the gods. The perfect man can put his whole soul upon that one point of love, yet he is unattached...The beggar is never happy...he never really enjoys what he gets...Be, therefore, not a beggar; be unattached."

Let me rephrase this quote, using language relevant to writers.

We want readers to love us. We love the power of throwing our whole soul upon our books, losing ourselves in our stories and letting the book become representative of who we are. The prolific writer can put all of his or her energy into their books, yet be unattached to them. The less prolific writer cannot avoid attachment, and therefore cannot avoid misery. Be, therefore, a prolific writer. Be unattached.

Swami Vivekananda makes other crucial points, but if I were to push this analogy further, I would do him injustice.

But, suffice to say that in order to be truly prolific, you need to be attached to your work and be unattached at the same.

Isn't that an oxymoron? How the hell can you be attached to something, yet not be attached?

It means to do work that matters, and to do that work with all of your soul. Do the work for the sake of doing the work. If it doesn't bring you the money, fame, or readers you wanted, that's okay.

If you wake up the next morning and realize that a book is the wrong book and you should be writing another book, you should start working on the other book without expending any sadness for what you've already written.

Easy to say, hard to do.

Be Spirited About the Writing Process, Not Your Story

Most authors are attached to their books.

"My heroine is amazing."

"My story is a mind-bender."

"The plot is gripping, and it has never been done before."

I enjoy hearing authors gush about their stories. They worked hard on them.

Ask many of those same authors about the writing process, and you'll usually hear something like this.

"It was a battle, but I won."

"I poured every inch of my soul into editing."

"I never thought I'd finish the first draft. It was rough."

When writers say this kind of thing, I just shake my head. They glamorize the struggle of writing, which in my opinion, is a mistake.

You want to be prolific, right?

Let's say you want to write 100 books. Do you *really* want to write 100 books and struggle every time? Do you want every single novel to be a war against your soul and spirit?

No, that's just silly.

If you want to be prolific, learn to love the process of writing. Every piece of it. If you can't learn to love a particular part of the process, commit to eliminating it.

Otherwise, you're going to hate the part of your career where you're going to spend most of your hours: writing. Hate the process and you'll burn out. Fast.

Let me give you a personal example about how I learned to love the process. I don't like writing multiple drafts. I hate it, actually. It screws up my flow, and the time I spend revising is better spent writing. Yet, early on in my career, many of my novels were three to four drafts, which drove me crazy. I committed to reducing my drafts down to two, and then, finally, one. I get everything right in the first draft, and then move on to the next novel. Now I love the process much more.

Be passionate about the process of writing. You must learn to love it. If you love the process of writing, you'll be amazed how much readers will love your characters because your passion will show in your writing.

Remember that! Just remember to be unattached.

———

Recap

- Being prolific comes from adopting the right mindset. The right mindset is one in which you understand what motivates you, what fills your spiritual and creative well, and what gives you peace about being an author. Every day you sit down to write, you must align yourself with that mindset.
- "Doing the work" must be enough for you.
- Don't compare yourself to others. It will only cause you pain and misery.
- Use your own personal experience as the basis for any expectations you set for yourself. If you must set *any* expectations for yourself, use these: write every day, you will not compare yourself to others, you will improve your skills with every new book, and you will have fun.
- Be attached and unattached to your work at the same time.
- Be spirited about the process of writing, not your story.

These steps are hard to master, but mastering them will advance you so far ahead in your career it won't even be funny.

Again, I don't believe in any of that woo-woo mindset stuff that other people write about, but if you want to be a long-term, prolific author, developing a healthy mindset is the critical first step. At least it was for me.

Now it's time to move from the land of philosophy into the land of action.

Essential Tools for Prolific Writers

Hopefully, you've connected with your purpose and adopted the right mindset, but that's only the first step. The next key to successful writing is having the right tools.

Imagine a watchmaker. She can't build the best watches by using a different set of tools every time. Not consistently.

As a writer and an artisan of the highest quality, you too must find your tools. And you must master them.

I'm going to share some tools that have helped me write fast and smart.

Scrivener iOS - The Secret to My Success

Enough has been written about Scrivener that I don't need to extol its virtues here.

But the iOS version was a game-changer.

Before Scrivener iOS, I was tied to my laptop. Any time I wanted to write something, I had to sit down at my laptop and write. I could go to a coffee shop, but even then, I had to bring my laptop, backpack, a mouse, and a charger. Oh, the horrors!

Scrivener iOS puts all of my manuscripts on the one device that I have with me at all times throughout the day: my phone. I can write new words, edit those words, and sync them up so that I can access them on my laptop later.

Again, game-changer.

But surprisingly, at least at the time of this writing, most writers haven't switched to mobile writing.

A couple of reasons: most people are scared of writing on their phone because the keyboard either feels weird or the process itself doesn't feel "quite right."

I understand that.

It was weird for me at first too, but I quickly got over it.

Now approximately 30-40% of all of my written words come from my phone.

Let me say that again in another way: 30-40% of my writing is done on my phone.

In case you still didn't see it, let's try again: since adopting Scrivener iOS, I have increased my word counts by 30-40%.

For those wondering, the amount of words written on my laptop remained the same. Scrivener iOS allowed me to add *new* words.

Being able to write on your phone frees up time for writing that you didn't know you had.

For example, let me give you some personal examples of writing sessions I've had within the last year:

- We only have one computer in my house. So if I'm writing and my wife needs to research something, I have to stop writing. With Scrivener, I just sync my work-in-progress to my phone and continue writing my novel on the couch. Once, I wrote over 1,000 words while waiting for my wife to do something on the computer.

- My wife *loves* shopping. I don't. Yet, I always find myself in department stores wanting to jump out the window. Whenever this happens, I find a nearby couch (there are plenty in department stores), sit down, and pick up where I left off in my book.
- I had to go renew my driver's license. I wanted to get to the bureau office early because the lines fill up quickly. Due to light traffic, I arrived about 15 minutes early. I wrote a couple hundred words while sitting in the car.
- I attend law school at night. I am good about doing my homework prior to class, so I write on my phone while waiting for class to begin.
- I write on breaks at work (and during lunch) and can usually write a couple hundred words per session.
- At work, I travel for business often. When I can, I write my novels while sitting around at the airport, on the plane, in the hotel room after a long day of work.
- When I'm sick, the last place I want to be is in front of my computer. Sometimes I can't even get out of bed. So I write in bed. Even if it's just a couple hundred words at a time, it adds up and I can keep momentum (yes, I write when I'm sick if possible).
- I've written a *lot* of words in the backseat of an Uber car.

I could go on and on.

The point is that writing on my phone has opened up a crazy amount of opportunities for me to be productive. It makes writing possible where it wasn't previously.

Think about that.

Even if you could only write 500 extra words per day on your phone, that would net you 182,500 words per year. That's nearly 4 novels at 50,000 words. And that's on TOP of what you write at your computer. Daaaaamn.

Yes, you'll have to figure out how to write on your phone. And yes, it's not the same.

But you'll get used to it.

I've been doing this for two years, and my wrists don't hurt and I don't have any medical complications.

Let me show you some more numbers.

Here's a breakdown of how many novels I wrote between 2013 and 2017.

> *2013: 1 novel (110,000 words)*
> *2014: 2 novels (140,000 words)*
> *2015: 4 novels (182,000 words)*
> *2016: 5 novels (270,000 words) —adopted mobile*
>   *writing mid-year and spent the year learning it*
> *2017: 13 novels (493,000 words)*

These numbers don't count my nonfiction titles, which were also written during this period.

Here's the story:

- I found my rhythm in 2016. If my lifestyle continued the way it did and I had the same amount of time to write, I would have probably plateaued around 4-5 novels with around 250,000 words per year. That's not a bad way to live, and most authors would probably be happy with this level of production.
- After adopting phone-based writing sessions, I more doubled my novel count from 5 to 13 and increased

the amount of words written by 82%! In one year. And I'm still getting faster. I haven't reached my peak yet.

- A couple hundred words per session make a big difference.

If you still need convincing, here are some qualitative observations:

- My initial worry about writing on my phone was quality, since I'm writing with my thumbs. I did a test. My editor is very familiar with my work and has historically told me that I write pretty clean manuscripts. So I wrote a novel entirely on my phone and I sent it to her without telling her that I wrote it on my phone. She didn't even notice a difference, and the amount of typos and spelling errors was comparable to what I typically produce on my laptop.
- Readers rarely call out typos or errors in my books. That hasn't changed. After all, the books are being edited just the same.
- I can usually write a couple hundred words in a sitting.
- On days where I am particularly busy and stressed, writing on my phone allows me to set micro goals. Just before I wrote this book, I fell ill with the flu, and I could not bring myself to write. But because I didn't want to lose daily momentum, I told myself I would write just 100 words per day. I did it easily and was able to keep momentum on the novel I was writing.

So there you have it. Little numbers here and there add up

in a big way. All it takes is a willingness to adopt this method, which, in my opinion, is far more practical than dictation (more on that next).

If you're a part-time author, writing on your phone is an especially important tool that you can use to keep the words flowing.

If you're a parent, writing on your phone is a godsend because you're never in one place for very long.

If you're a full-time author, writing on your phone will make you even more dangerous than you already are.

Basically, if you have a smart phone, hands, and an absence of medical issues that could get in the way, phone-based writing is a tool that prolific authors of the 21st century can adopt in order to be more productive.

The tool matters. Besides Scrivener, there are other writing apps out there, such as Ulysses, which is a fantastic writing app in its own right. You'll have to do research based on what type of phone operating system you have. There are plenty of apps out there, but they're not all created equal unfortunately. But if you can find a way to write novels on your phone, you will be amazed how much more productive you can be.

What We Speak of When We Speak of Dictation

I would be remiss not to talk about dictation.

In recent years, a lot of people have turned to it as a reliable way to produce more words.

We speak faster than we write, so it's logical that dictation is a tool that prolific writers should consider.

I like dictation. I used it to write my *Last Dragon Lord* series. If you can get over the learning curve, it's a fantastic tool.

As great of a tool as dictation is, there are a couple of problems with it that you have to think about.

First, you are still tied to your computer, unless you use an app like Dragon Anywhere.

Second, writing software has a long way to go before it will be dictation-friendly. Programs like Dragon do a good job of trying to play nice, but there are a lot of glitches still and it is easy to lose words.

Third, you can use transcription, but it's messy and expensive.

From a consistency perspective, dictation is just not reliable enough for me to sustain on a regular basis. I need a fast, systematic, and reliable way to produce words every day, and dictation doesn't do that for me. Maybe it will do that for you, though, which is why I wanted to talk about it.

If you pair it with phone-based writing, it can be a powerful way to grow your word count.

There have been plenty of books and videos on dictation that I won't write any further about it.

What Gets Measured Gets Managed

It's not enough just to write every day. You also need to keep track of your word counts to look for trends and ways to improve your process.

Scrivener will track your daily count for you automatically. Before that, I tracked my word counts in Microsoft Excel.

It can be a burden sometimes, but it's crucial to track your words. It doesn't take very long, and doing it will give you some historical insight into the evolution of your writing speed. If you track it right, you can even track your word counts at each point in your novels and compare novels against each other.

For example, does your word count trail off every time you reach the "final battle?" Do you write more words every time there is a love scene? That's useful information.

Your goal should be to find a reliable tool to help you measure and track your daily, monthly, and yearly word count. How granular you want to go with it is entirely up to you.

———

Recap

- Phone-based writing has allowed me to increase my writing dramatically. It can do the same for you. It's still a relatively new trend.
- Dictation can help you get to higher word counts.
- Set up a reliable way to track your word counts.

Master these tools because you will be using them for your entire career.

Time Management: Master It or Fail

Once you've mastered your tools, it's time to master your time.

Time management is important, but sometimes when people talk about it, they get into woo-woo territory, so I'm going to say all I need to say in a couple of paragraphs.

You're either devoting time to your writing or you're diverting time away from it.

Also, family is important. Don't neglect your family.

Other things, however, aren't nearly as important. For example, I stopped watching television in order to support my writing habit.

Giant, interrupted blocks of time are unrealistic for most people. Whenever possible, it's far better to have smaller blocks of focused time. Those blocks add up and as a whole are often more productive than big 3 or 4-hour writing sessions.

You have to decide at the macro level what you're going to start, stop, and continue. Figure out what your daily writing cadence is.

Find Your Cadence

. . .

Here are the decisions I made at the macro level early on in my career.

I stopped watching movies and television. I also stopped playing video games forever in 2012.

I cut back on my reading. Before publishing my first book, I read around 100 books per year. I cut back considerably on that number, but I still read regularly, as that's just good for business.

I stopped hanging out with certain friends whom I had grown apart from. I know this might sound cold, but I decided that I preferred to spend free time by myself instead of with other people. Not all of the time, but most of the time. I've never been one to have many friends, so I keep to myself and keep a laser-like focus on my writing.

I gave up my hobby of writing music.

I sold damn near everything I owned that took away my focus on writing.

The result of all those things is a daily cadence that looks something like this:

> *5:30 AM: Wake up and take a shower*
> *6:00-7:30 AM: Write on my laptop (1,000-2,000*
>   *words)*
> *7:30-10:30 AM: Commute and work*
> *10:30-10:45 AM: Break at work (200-300 words)*
> *10:45-12:00 PM: Work*
> *12:00-12:45 PM: Lunch with my wife*
> *12:45-1:00 PM: Write more words (200-300 words)*
> *1:00-2:30 PM: Work*
> *2:30-2:45 PM: Break at work (200-300 words)*
> *2:45-5:00 PM: Work and commute*
> *5:00-8:00 PM: Family time or law school class time*

> *8:00-9:30 PM: Write on my laptop (1,000-2,000 words) or do law school homework*
> *9:30 PM: Bedtime*

This is my writing schedule Monday through Friday most days. I don't wake up early on weekends, but I still write whenever I can.

This daily cadence results in approximately 2,600 to 4,600 words per day, though honestly, I spend a good number of days north of 5,000. I don't consider this to be an incredible number, though some might. There are authors who make me look like a snail.

You don't need to write 10,000 words per day to be prolific. That's a myth.

You can develop an incredible career writing small amounts of words every day. Just do the daily, weekly, monthly, and yearly math. It will surprise you.

The key is consistency. If you can develop momentum and keep it going, the words will take care of themselves.

If you can develop a cadence, you'll ensure that you create time for the words to flow.

If you can't develop a cadence, that's okay too. You just need to be aware of it and be more vigilant about finding pockets of time and seizing them when you do.

There are weeks when school or work takes over my life and I have to make the best of that. There are weeks where things at work and school are fine, but my personal life is busy. I've learned to go with the flow and find harmony between the different areas of my life as best as I can.

Don't believe any of that crap about work-life balance. Balance implies that you have to divide up your time equally. As a father, employee, son, and writer, that's next to impossible. My sole focus has been in ensuring that the different spheres of my life play well together. This keeps me flexible. Harmony is what you want.

Look for Pockets of Time

Train yourself to look for pockets of time to write during the day. Always be asking yourself, "Can I write something right now?"

A few words of caution.

It's not a good idea to ignore your family (I'll say it until you believe me!).

It's also not a good idea to write when you're supposed to be working. I built my successful writing empire while also being successful at work as a manager at a Fortune 100 insurance company. When I'm at work, I work. When I'm on my own time, I use it wisely.

Don't be antisocial, especially if you write on your phone. Don't miss out (too much) on meaningful interactions with people. Pay attention to your surroundings. That's just good writer behavior.

But…

Can you find pockets of time?

Here are places I've found it: home, relatives' houses, doctor's office, dentist's office, driver's license bureau, department store, grocery store, tailor, the mall, the airport, the bus terminal, coffee shop, park, backseat of an Uber car, on the bus, standing around in random places waiting for random things, on hold with call centers, while watching YouTube webinars, laundromats…

The list goes on and on.

How bad do you really want this?

———

Recap

- Time management is another essential skill of prolific authors. If you want to develop this skill, you need to be in the top 1% of people when it comes to managing your time. Sometimes that means cutting some things (and people) out of your life. Sometimes it means being a jerk to protect your time.
- Make high-level decisions on what you're going to start, stop, and continue.
- Find and hone your daily cadence. Don't fret your daily word count—consistency is the key.
- Look for pockets of time wherever you can find them, and when you find them, USE THEM!

Congratulations. I've taught you the three cornerstone skills that you will put you well on your way to writing faster and smarter.

Writing Smart

If you want to be prolific, then you have to learn to write smart.

"Write smart" means different things for every author. There is no single strategy that will make you prolific overnight. You have to find what is right for you.

I recommend that writers always look for process improvements in how they work. When I started writing, it took me a year to write my first novel. Now I can write a novel in a month or less. That saved time goes toward more novels, marketing and promotion, and other general business tasks that require my attention.

I've tried a lot of things to shave time off novels. Some of them worked, others exploded in my face. I'll share the ideas that worked in this chapter.

I will warn you that these ideas are not the typical writing advice. They're going to make you feel uncomfortable initially. But if you can learn them, you'll zoom so far ahead in your writing that you won't be able to believe it. The tips in this section are the reason I woke up four years into my writing career simply stunned at how far I had come.

If you find yourself immediately repulsed by one of these ideas, that means you should probably try it. That's your inner critic overreacting to something that your subconscious probably likes!

Outlining: Give It Up

Writers love outlining. It's one of the few idols that we pray to in this profession. Writers love to organize their outlines, make them look nice and pretty, color code them, and deck them out with character sheets and timelines and all other kinds of bells and whistles.

I did all that stuff. I was no exception early in my career.

But outlining sucks more time out of the writing process than I care to spare.

I did a time audit a few years back. I tracked how long it took me (to the minute) to write an entire trilogy.

Here is the breakdown of how long each part of the writing process took:

> *20% outlining (8 hours)*
> *60% writing first draft (24 hours)*
> *20% writing subsequent drafts (8 hours)*
> *40 hours total*

Out of 40 hours, only 24 of them were actually spent writing.

40 hours is a typical work week.

Would your boss be happy if you only produced work 24 hours out of the week?

When you're writing, you're in production.

When you're not writing, you're not in production.

It's that simple.

Any time spent not writing words is time that you can't count.

You can't count outlining in your word count. You can't count marketing either. You have to find other time to do those things, and whether you like it or not, that time has to come from your writing time.

If you want to increase your output, you have to focus on maximizing your time. With outlining, I got tired of having days where I didn't write a single word, yet worked on revising my outline. Those days felt empty to me, like I could have spent them more wisely.

The fact that I spent 20% of my time outlining irritated me. Nine times out of ten, my books veered away from the original outline. In the case of my trilogy, it happened with all three books. And when I say I deviated from the outline, I consistently deviated at the chapter level.

If I was spending all this time outlining, why wasn't it accurate? If I didn't end up following the outline, why the hell was I doing it?

So I stopped.

Boom--8 hours back, just like that. Was it easy? No. It required me to think differently, and the first couple novels I wrote without outlining took me longer in the beginning. But now, I don't miss outlining (at all), and my stories are better because of it.

Giving up outlines is like taking the training wheels off your bike for the first time. You fall down a lot and you scrape your knee a couple of times, but as long as you wear a helmet and keep trying, you'll be okay.

I write this knowing that many, many authors are going to be mad at me for saying it. As I said before, I'm throwing a trusted idol out the window.

Giving up outlines is next to impossible for many writers.

"But how do you know what happens next?"

"How do you know if your characters are deep enough?"

"What if your story doesn't conform to the Hero's Journey/Plot Point Theory/Save the Cat (or whatever)?"

"What if you write yourself into a corner that you can't get out of?"

Common questions from outliners.

The answer is that the story just works itself out. All you have to do is trust yourself and fight your fear along the way. Read the later section in this book about writer's block for a strategies on how I deal with writing without outlines. It can be done.

For a great book on writing without outlines, read Dean Wesley Smith's *Writing into the Dark*. It's the premier book on writing without an outline. Read it, then read it again.

Stopping outlining has numerous benefits:

- As Dean Wesley Smith frequently argues, if YOU don't know what's going to happen in your story, neither will your readers, and that's exciting.
- You save time and effort.
- You eliminate a frustration point. I can't tell you how many times I lost momentum during the outline phase before the story even started.

Give it a shot. Either one of two things will happen: you'll either fail and go back to outlining (which means you need to work on mindset and fear, and you're not ready yet) or you'll succeed and never need to do it again. In my opinion, it's worth the risk.

Revision: Skip It by Getting Your Story Right the First Time

. . .

That's right. Skip every draft but your first.

This advice contradicts the biggest bad habit (in my opinion) writers have. This habit is taught in schools, and it is spread on writer's blogs, podcasts, and writing books.

That habit is to write sloppy first drafts.

If you feel that it helps you, fine. But know that it's a crutch.

Truly prolific authors don't need to write multiple drafts. They get the story right the first time and move on.

Easy to say, hard to do, but if you can learn this skill, it will expand your horizon and open up so many more opportunities for you.

Going back to my time audit for my trilogy, 20% of my time was spent on subsequent drafts. That meant that I wrote a sloppy first draft and went back over it multiple times before calling it good.

When you're editing, you're not writing.

Some of my very worst emotional days during this trilogy were spent editing that first, second, and third draft. Honestly. I kept a writing journal, and the entries from those days are unbearable to read even now.

Writing sloppy first drafts is a bad habit for a number of reasons.

First, when you write sloppy, you have to spend time fixing silly mistakes. Sometimes in my first drafts, I would skip entire chapters, hoping the inspiration would strike me later. Or I would write skeleton battle scenes, returning to flesh them out later. Worst of all, I would put things in brackets, like [insert dialogue and description of villain here]. Very easy to do, and very destructive.

Why not just write it well the first time?

Second, sloppy drafts invite fear into your workspace. You

can't edit a first draft without jumping on the emotional roller-coaster. After all, you wrote a sloppy first draft. Why *wouldn't* you cringe when you reread it?

You also create a self-fulfilling prophecy that looks like this:

- You write a sloppy (i.e. shitty) first draft.
- You review that draft and realize that it is, in fact, shitty.
- That makes YOU feel like shit.
- Editing becomes a bear because you begin to doubt yourself and your ability.
- The entire editing process turns into an emotional rollercoaster, with you having to beat your fear and feeling of shittiness. Sure, you finish the story, but you come away feeling like it was a "struggle" or a "battle."
- (Optional) Some writers take a "mental" break from writing after finishing. That break usually lasts longer than it should.
- The process begins again, and you reinforce the bad habit.

This is why I don't advocate for writing multiple drafts.

I know too many writers who never escape that negative loop. The emotional rollercoaster is deadly. As someone who has a lot of "former writer" friends, trust me when I say it kills careers. Personally, I didn't like the highs and lows of that emotional rollercoaster, so I committed to cutting it out of my life. As you'll see in the Writer's Block section, I still have highs and lows, but they are much more reasonable since I dumped multiple drafts.

Also, I just don't *enjoy* revision in general. It's not fun for me.

Writing is fun. "Refining" and "revising" is not. Personal preference.

I decided that I'd rather take longer to write a first draft and eliminate the editing phase altogether. When I did this, I found that I actually wrote shorter first drafts. Funny how that works.

My process today is that I write one draft, get it right the first time, and then I send it to my editor.

Boom. Another 8 hours saved, with the added benefit of faster, more accurate first drafts. Everything I write goes to a professional editor, so it all comes out at the same level of quality anyway.

How do you *not* write sloppy first drafts, you ask? You can start by reading regularly, and studying bestselling authors to see how they write. You can also start by making a commitment to study the craft regularly, and imitate the techniques of the masters. All it takes is commitment. The more you write, the better you will get. You just have to be intentional about your development.

I won't lie to you and tell you this is easy. But if you are wanting to go on with the strategies in the rest of this book, I argue that they will be very hard to do if you outline and write multiple drafts.

Still not convinced? That's okay. Just keep this chapter in the back of your head, and be open to the idea of committing to a new way of writing when you're ready.

Stop Being a Perfectionist

This ties in with writing multiple drafts.

Writers are taught in school that we have to refine our work. Most of us have an image in our heads of that writer in his ivory tower, spending hours trying to find the right word, producing a single book every 10 years.

Push that image out of your mind.

Stop focusing on getting your manuscript perfect.

Focus on getting it done, and done right.

Will a reader notice if you spend 4 extra drafts on a book? Probably not. They're not going to come to your house and shoot you if they don't like your book. They will, however, send you an email and praise you if they like it.

Most writers I talk to object against my criticism of perfectionism.

"How do you know your readers will like a faster story?" they ask.

I usually reply, "You won't know until you try it."

Those writers are usually fearful of producing a substandard product, and I can understand that fear.

But substandard is usually not what happens.

Since adopting a faster writing style, the praise from my reviewers has gone up, not down.

Just remember that speed does not equal quality.

I'm not telling you to avoid editors or proofreaders. You need them.

But what you don't need is 15 drafts.

Learn how to focus on "good enough" and not perfect.

I know, I know, that goes against everything you've been taught, but if you keep down this road, your readers will thank you.

A great book on this topic is *The Pursuit of Perfection* by Kristine Kathryn Rusch.

Beta Readers: Bless Their Hearts, But You Don't Need Them

. . .

I have nothing against beta readers. They are wonderful people who volunteer their time to help authors write better books. While I could quibble a little bit about whether listening to your beta readers betrays your subconscious, I won't.

Here's the thing about beta readers: they do a good service, but they'll slow you down.

Beta readers are regular people like you and me. They don't read books for a living. Life gets in the way.

Unless you're particularly good at controlling them so that they meet your deadlines, chances are high that they will slow down your process because you're introducing an unknown time variable into the mix.

For that reason alone, you're better off relying on an editor.

If you *are* going to recruit a beta reader, pay them for their time so that you can command a firm deadline. But even then, you have to ask whether your money would be better spent on something else.

Remember, you want to avoid bottlenecks in your production. Beta readers too frequently cause a bottleneck.

Like I said, bless their hearts, but you don't need them.

————

Recap

- Writing smarter should always be your goal.
- My opinion of writing smart works for me. You have to find the strategy that works for you.
- What I will tell you is that history shows that the most prolific authors forwent most if not all of the things included in this chapter (outlining, revision, etc.). If you don't believe me, study the lives of the great pulp writers.
- History and experience are on my side. If you can

find another way, go for it, but know that any alternative path you take will probably lead you back here.

- Commit to writing smart. The time and effort you devote in this category will pay for themselves in the long run.

Writer's Block Part 1: How to Beat It Every Time

Ah, the dreaded writer's block.

No writing book would be complete without addressing it.

Before we continue, let me make a controversial disclaimer. And unlike in my mindset chapter, I *am* going to get woo-woo for a moment...

I don't like the term "writer's block." I hate it, actually.

Let's define "writer's block": in my opinion, it's the author's inability to write the next word in their story because of an emotional or creative interruption. I believe that "writer's block" can stop you from writing your next chapter, or it can be like the flu infecting you as you write, making you feel like you're not writing anything of value.

Here's why I don't like "writer's block" and everything associated with it.

It's too much of an excuse. When you utter the words, it's almost like you're giving yourself permission not to write. The world understands you too, and they grant you that permission. Most non-writers have a mental image in their heads of a writer with writer's block, wandering around with a fatigued look on their face, trying to think of the right phrase to put in a paragraph. It's a romantic association that most people have of writers. I believe we should do whatever we can do avoid those kind of romantic associations.

Let me tell you what "writer's block" really is.

"Writer's block" is your subconscious measuring out and managing your interactions with the universe.

Before you run away screaming and accusing me of being a crazy hippie, let me explain myself...

Your Subconscious is the Key to Everything

Have you ever thought about your subconscious?

I don't have a psychology degree, so what I'm about to explain isn't going to be scientifically accurate, but it *is* going to be true to my own experience.

Most of us write from our conscious. We write our stories, edit them, and make all creative decisions consciously.

However, all ideas and inspiration actually come from the subconscious. And your subconscious is a powerful thing. All the answers you need in life are floating around in your subconscious, and if you want to access them, all you have to do is ask for them. Additionally, your subconscious is always paying attention to your surroundings.

Your conscious is like a stern parent.

Your subconscious is like an optimistic child.

When you're writing, you need to let that optimistic child out and kick the parent out of the house. The child is where the creativity comes from. The parent shuts down your creativity because it focuses on logic, which doesn't play well with inspiration.

There are plenty of ways to describe this relationship, many of which you've heard before. Some call it left brain and right brain. Some people call the conscious the "inner critic" and the subconscious "the muse." Dean Wesley Smith calls the subconscious the creative voice and the conscious the critical voice.

You get the picture.

The point is that you need to trust your subconscious and let it guide you through the writing process. When you do, nothing can stop you.

But what about "writer's block," you ask?

Again, the definition: "writer's block" is your subconscious measuring out and managing your interactions with the universe.

When you experience "writer's block," it's because your subconscious has encountered a problem and needs help solving it.

Think about a lab rat negotiating a labyrinth in order to find cheese at the end. Every once in a while, it comes to a dead end. But it uses its nose and intuition to find its way to the end of the course. Sometimes it has to backtrack; other times it has to change direction. Sometimes it has to jump over or go through obstacles.

Your books are the labyrinth, and your subconscious is the lab rat.

Your role in the process is to listen deeply and figure out how to redirect that inner lab rat to the cheese.

This is why I don't like the term "writer's block." It's too passive. It doesn't just go away on its own, but we act as if we'll simply wake up one day and the writer's block will be gone. Most times—9 times out of 10—it requires active participation from the writer. As a culture, we don't do enough to promote that.

Also, I don't like the term "writer's block" because it is

counterintuitive to being prolific. Prolific writers write book after book. Writers who believe in "writer's block" allow it to become a regular occurrence. It's like that friend who comes over once a week and overstays their welcome, and you don't say anything because you don't want to be mean.

There really is no better word to replace the term, honestly. At least not in English. It's a feeling, a co-existence with your subconscious, not something you can truly define. So for the sake of explaining my reasoning, I'll continue using the term "writer's block", but just know that I do it reluctantly.

Here's a noble theory: I will make the argument that "writer's block" is helpful to the writing process IF you use it properly.

Think about the last time you experienced a block. It was probably agonizing, and you didn't write for days. But when you finally got over it, the novel flowed. If you look back at your novel now, after distance and time, the rough patches probably look and feel seamless. In fact, your readers probably wouldn't even notice that you struggled with those sections.

Have you ever considered that maybe the "writer's block" was exactly what your novel needed at that point in time?

I know, I know, that's controversial.

Instead of exerting your energy *fighting* the "writer's block," what if you leaned into it instead? What if you treated it as a partnership with your subconscious? What if you could figure out what your subconscious needed, give that to your subconscious, and then continue your work-in-progress?

Believe it or not, there are tricks to do this. Many of them are in this section.

Obstacles will always be a regular occurrence in your writing career, but the simple mindset shifts in this chapter will help you rechannel your energy and make "writer's block" one of the most critical secrets to your success.

. . .

How to Use This Section

I have grouped this section into several parts:

- Reasons You Get Stuck
- General Maintenance Strategies to Keep You Motivated
- Strategies to Combat Lack of Inspiration
- Strategies to Combat Fear

Those strategies are broken into smaller, quick hit chapters that will teach you a strategy, give you some additional things to consider, and some examples.

Over the last few years, I've developed these strategies to ensure that I move through my books at a consistent pace, even if I don't feel like writing on a particular day.

This is the most important section in the book, because I'm going to teach you everything I know about starting and finishing novels without getting hung up too much with "writer's block."

Read these strategies, pick out the ones that resonate most with you, and adapt them for your own needs. You may also want to bookmark this section so you can come back to it later, as not all of the strategies will be useful for your current project, but they might be a few books down the road.

Ultimately, the goal here is to show you just how flexible you need to be in order to be prolific.

As a writer, I will bet that you have no problem coming up with ideas. Creativity is what you do, right? Most authors accept the fact that they will never be able to write down all the ideas in their heads.

For me, thinking of new ideas in my stories is like jazz

improvisation. I go with the flow, and I can always count on a new idea forming just in time, whenever I need it.

How creative are you when it comes to the writing process?

When you hit a snag in your work in progress, can you improv just as well and fast in thinking of ways to break through the issue?

If not, that's okay. It's a skill you can learn.

Just remember: if you can come up with a lot of ideas for your book, you can come up with just as many ideas to speed through blocks. All it takes is practice.

Reasons You Get Stuck

Lack of Inspiration

There are only a couple reasons your subconscious needs help.

The first (and most common) issue is that it needs inspiration. Your subconscious knows where your story needs to go and what your characters need to do. However, it needs an event to draw from in order to feed you the next scene. So it waits.

This is why the common advice to "keep your eyes and ears open" as a writer is important. When you are always on the lookout for things to write about, you can minimize this kind of blockage. If you're always feeding your subconscious a steady stream of data points, it won't need as much help in this area and your time in the rough patches will be shorter.

Here's an example from my writing. In my book, *Android Deception*, I hit a rough patch around the middle and wasn't sure how to proceed. I listened to myself and tried to figure out what my subconscious needed.

I needed some inspiration. My wife and I ended up going

to a local bakery that I had never been to before. It was exactly what I needed. I remember taking in the sights and smells of the place, watching the people eating their croissants and drinking their coffee. I remember the sound of spoons clinking against mugs.

I remember thinking, "How would I describe this place if I wrote it in a novel?" When I got home, I wrote that bakery into the next scene, which was where I needed one of my characters to go. Once I figured that out, my subconscious took care of the rest and powered onward as usual. The bakery was the missing link. That scene ended up being one of most memorable in the book.

Ironically, I don't believe this was a coincidence. I believe my subconscious knew I was going to go to that local bakery and be inspired from it.

What I don't want you to take away from this book is that everything in your life is predestined and that what will happen will happen no matter what you do. Human nature will cause some people reading to think "Writer's block is okay. I'll just wait it out." That's not okay.

What I *do* want you to take away is that life is fluid. Things are ever-changing. Your mindset matters and your choices matter. If you make the commitment and promise to yourself that you will listen to your subconscious and do what it needs, then you can speed things up.

If I hadn't been as self-aware while writing *Android Deception*, maybe the "writer's block" would have lasted longer for me and I wouldn't have written the bakery scene. But the subconscious's need would have been the same. What might have happened instead is that I would have visited another place that triggered my emotions and ended up using that in the story instead. Or I might have seen an exotic locale on television that triggered some sort of inspiration. The bakery might have become a church, or a desert, or whatever. I would have picked up on the clue eventually, though I wouldn't have necessarily realized that my subconscious needed it. I would have chalked it up as a coincidence and moved on, not understanding the root cause of the "writer's block" to begin with. But the point is that I would have overcome the issue eventually, and the universe would have molded itself around my choices. All of those potential paths the novel could have taken would have been perfectly valid, not good or bad.

Again, life is fluid. Time flows. You are exactly where you need to be in life, but the only way you stay there is to continue making good choices. And in this case, good choices come from being aware of your surroundings and knowing how to trigger inspiration at a moment's notice.

Fear

The second reason the subconscious gets stuck is fear.

To be clear, your subconscious is not scared.

Your subconscious is fearless.

Usually, when fear is involved, your conscious is standing in the subconscious's way, preventing you from seeing clearly.

In order to fight fear, you have to understand where it comes from. Then you can use the strategies in this section to disarm it.

Fear is ever-shifting and relentless.

There's the fear of inadequacy, that feeling that you don't have the skills to finish your next book or you won't measure up to other authors.

There's the fear of rejection, that readers will not read your book or will laugh at you.

There's the fear of abandonment, that readers won't read the rest of the books in your series.

There's the fear of misperception, that people won't understand something in your story. That could cause shame, humiliation, or feelings that you aren't worthy.

And if you want to get really complicated, there's the fear of money—that feeling that your book won't make money, so what's the point. Really deadly. That fear usually comes from past sales numbers.

There's paranoia, that feeling that you won't live long enough to finish your book, or someone else will write your story and do it better.

There's the fear of success too, believe it or not.

And we haven't even gotten into external fears, like the fear of losing your job or conflicts with a spouse, issues with a loved one, and so on.

There are many, many kinds of fear. Not all fears involve your writing, but almost all of them will affect it.

When you hit a rough patch, sometimes there is one fear driving your issues; other times it can be multiple fears. Sometimes the fear has nothing to do with your work at all.

Your job is to isolate the fear, figure out where it is coming from, and eliminate it.

Life Events

Life is all about harmony. Every person's definition of harmony is different, but I believe that all of us are striving toward harmony of some kind.

Your subconscious knows this. After all, writing your novel isn't its only responsibility. It's also responsible for leading you through life.

And sometimes, there are other things in your life that have to take priority over your writing.

Here's an example to help illustrate this.

First, while I was writing *this very book*, I sat down to write, but my mind kept pulling me out of the book. Initially, it frustrated me. But when I figured out why, I discovered it had nothing to do with fear.

Later that day, I received an email regarding my taxes that derailed my entire afternoon and evening. I had to take care of it. I rechanneled my energy and focused on the tax issue, resolving it later that night. Once I was done, I sat down to write, and my subconscious picked up at full speed. Funny how that works.

It knew that I had to deal with this tax issue, so it put the brakes on my words.

I could have chosen to continue writing and ignored the tax issue. And I might have been okay. But I might have created a bigger problem for myself down the road that would have taken me away from my writing for an even greater length of time. So in my opinion, it's far better to listen to yourself.

Also, let's not forget that life happens. People die. People get injured. People get sick. This could happen to you, or it could happen to one of your loved ones. When this happens, put the writing on hold and do what you have to do. Don't feel guilty about it. Start back up when you can. When you do, your subconscious will be waiting for you. Unfortunately, I can't offer any strategies to combat this other than to do what you have to do.

The only danger with this kind of problem is misdiagnosing it and devolving into procrastination. Things will come up in your life all the time, but that doesn't mean that it's an excuse to procrastinate. As you learn to listen, you will get better at avoiding procrastination.

Remember, you're striving for harmony. Sometimes your writing will have to flex in order to reach it. Everything averages out in the grand scheme of things.

. . .

Bringing It All Together

Lack of inspiration, fear, and life events are really the only three reasons your subconscious gets stuck. If we wanted to be scientific, we could break these down further, but most problems you will encounter will probably fall into one of these three categories.

If you want to be successful in minimizing "writer's block," then focus on being in tune to what your subconscious needs.

Writer's Block Part 2: General Maintenance Strategies to Keep You Motivated

There are a number of things you can do on a regular basis to ensure that your subconscious doesn't get stuck.

Think of the strategies in this section like general maintenance for your writing mind, like changing the oil in your car, or checking the tire pressure, or changing the windshield wipers. These strategies are good for all seasons, and I recommend that you learn how to master most of them. I use many of these strategies daily, and in most cases, they have either completely eliminated "writer's block" or minimized it to almost nothing.

I use these strategies first. When they don't work, then I resort to the remaining strategies in the Lack of Inspiration and Fear sections.

Strategy #1: Ask Yourself the Tough Questions, Then Be Quiet and Listen

The first general maintenance strategy calls for introspection.

Have you ever asked yourself a question?

Have you ever had a conversation with yourself?

So many people I know don't take time for introspection. They claim they "don't have time" for it, or that it seems silly, or that "only weird people do that."

Introspection isn't weird, and it's definitely something you should make time for.

In order to determine where your subconscious is and what kind of help it needs, you need to ask.

Here's how I usually do it. Whenever I am stuck and feel a block coming on, I close my eyes and ask myself one of the following questions:

"What do I need to continue in my story?"

"What's blocking me right now, and what can I do about it?"

"How do I solve this?"

For maximum effect, I ask myself these questions when I am in the shower, driving to work, or falling asleep.

Now, on to answers.

Most people might think that your subconscious will jump up and down and tell you what you need.

"I need you to drink some coffee, please!"

"I need you to have a conversation with the next random stranger you meet!"

"Would you mind taking a nap?"

Unfortunately, it doesn't work that way. Your subconscious doesn't answer questions clearly. The answer will never come to you right away. And it will never come in the format you're expecting.

Also, you have to learn how to silence all the other chattering thoughts in your head. Sometimes they speak so loudly that you can't hear what your subconscious is trying to tell you.

You must learn to identify your subconscious's voice. You'll know it when you hear it. It's not so much a voice as it is a feeling. When you connect with it, you'll feel it guiding you and sometimes controlling your mind as you write.

When the answer comes, you will know. For me, a random thought will usually pop into my head that will solve the issue I'm having. I call it a glimmer—suddenly, I "see" a way forward in my story, and my mind expands ever so slightly.

I've learned to be on the lookout for glimmers, and I love that moment when they appear. It gives me a satisfying feeling, like leveling up does in a video game.

Asking the tough questions simply tells your subconscious that you know it needs help. When you do, your subconscious begins a negotiation with the universe to try to figure out how it can proceed.

I heard a saying once that no question ever goes unanswered. Ask a question to the universe, and it will answer you in its own way.

You just have to be quiet and listen.

Strategy #2: Meditate

Enough has been written about the medical and spiritual benefits of meditation that I won't summarize them here.

But I will talk about how you can use meditation as a writer.

Meditation is the perfect way to ask yourself questions. It's also the perfect way for you to learn how to listen to yourself.

Meditation is easy too. Find a quiet room, a comfortable chair, set a timer, sit down, and close your eyes.

Once, at a teenage boy's camp, my counselor facilitated a devilish exercise to show us just how disconnected we were from nature.

He told us to close our eyes and be silent for one minute.

At the end of the minute, we were told to raise our hands.

I'll never forget what happened next. I closed my eyes and became aware of the train wreck going on inside my head. I could not shut my mind off. The inside of my head was filled with sights, sounds, and smells. I was *itchy* and I fought the urge to scratch my face. I remembered things that I forgot to pack. I tried to count to 60, but I lost focus.

I ended up raising my hand, not knowing how much time

had passed.

I opened my eyes, and other boys were grinning at me with their hands up. Others still had their eyes closed, mental anguish clearly visible on their faces.

My counselor stood there with a stopwatch and a smirk on his face, waiting for everyone to raise their hands.

About 2 minutes later, everyone finished.

He then told us that the first person raised their hand after 30 seconds, and the last person raised their hand at 2 minutes.

I raised mine somewhere around 40 seconds…

That was eye-opening for me.

You see, we don't always have a true concept of time. With technology and our fast-paced lives, we live quickly, which disconnects us with time and, most importantly, our inner selves.

Meditation helps you reconnect with yourself. It's one of the few things that you can do every day and see incredible mental, spiritual, and health improvements quickly.

I'm not advocating that you meditate for hours at a time.

I meditate for five minutes every morning, just before I write.

I sit in my recliner in my office, set a timer on my phone, and close my eyes.

I ask myself, "Where was I in my work-in-progress?" (Or, I ask myself one of the tough questions in the last strategy.)

The most recent scene in my story flashes in my mind's eye.

Then I sit still and listen to my subconscious answer. Sometimes it will show me what's next. Other times it will be silent and I can focus on clearing my mind of any clutter.

In any case, the goal is to go with the flow.

When my timer goes off, I'm at complete peace. I can usually start writing quickly after my meditation sessions.

Daily meditation is good for your mind. It's a lubricant that keeps your subconscious operating without friction.

Strategy #3: When in Doubt, Listen to Your Subconscious

The old adage is true: listen to your gut.

This is good advice for every area of your life, but it's especially helpful when you're writing your story.

When you come to a decision in your story, and there are multiple paths and you can't quite decide what to do, it's always a good idea to listen to your subconscious. It usually will steer you in one direction over the other.

Try to avoid thinking logically about your problem. Instead, listen to where your subconscious is pointing you.

For example, in my dark fantasy series *The Last Dragon Lord*, my main character is a blood-thirsty, narcissistic dragon. When I conceived the series, I wanted to give him a love interest. I could see her very clearly in my mind. But when I sat down to write the story, my subconscious led me in the opposite direction. I struggled with this one because what I was writing conflicted with what I originally planned. I started thinking (against the wishes of my subconscious) about how I could logically insert the love interest into the story. After listening, I decided that my subconscious likely changed direction and didn't feel like telling me. I ditched all thoughts of a love inter-est, and thank God I did because the story was better for it.

The temptation when you arrive at these kind of crossroads is to think your way out of the problem. That's dangerous because you invite the inner critic (and fear) into your story. You'll create more problems for yourself if you do that.

Sometimes, when you're writing, the way forward will branch in different directions, and each direction will seem like a valid choice.

Let your subconscious be your compass. Make the decision as quickly as you can and move on.

Strategy #4: Read Regularly

Reading books regularly is a sure-fire way to keep your creative well full.

It doesn't matter what you read. Just do it.

Reading is as sacred as writing.

Most writers I know start off as avid readers. When they decide to become writers, the reading drops off because the writing requires so much time and energy. After all, authors have to write their stories, edit them, format them, market them, promote them, do taxes, track their sales, write newsletters, work with cover designers and editors, and so on. The list never ends. A writer's time is always under siege, and it's easy to stop reading.

I myself am no exception to this rule. While I still read books, my reading habits are less consistent. I used to read two to three books a week. Now I'm lucky if I can read one.

Reading fills the creative well because it gives the subconscious reference points for characters, story, and dialogue.

It would be impossible to imagine a musician who doesn't listen to music, a painter who doesn't study paintings, or an actor who doesn't watch plays. Just as those artists study their craft, so too must writers.

I know, it's hard.

But if you do it regularly, your subconscious will thank you.

There are so many ways to consume books these days that there's no excuse not to find some time.

There's another benefit to reading. Dean Wesley Smith, one of the most prolific writers writing today, often talks about how reading gives your subconscious permission to use new tools. Your subconscious has all the tools is needs to tell a story; it just needs permission to use them. Reading is how you do that. I agree with Dean on this, and I have found it to be true for me.

I do most of my reading on my phone. Ebooks are a godsend for me. I also have an Audible membership and listen to audiobooks during my commute. I listen to them at two times or three times speed so I can get through them faster.

Find a reading style that suits your lifestyle. If you like paperbacks, read paperbacks. If you're constantly on the go like me, then maybe ebook and audio are best. The key is to read.

Reading today is the best way to prevent a block tomorrow.

Strategy #5: Keep an Idea Log

Do you have a reliable system to capture ideas when you encounter them?

Let's say you're on a walk with your significant other, and during the course of a chat, a brilliant idea for a new steampunk series pops into your head. How do you capture it so that it doesn't fade away?

I keep what I call an "idea log."

I've been doing this ever since I was a teenager. I used to carry pocket-size notebooks around in my pocket along with a mini pencil so that I could write down ideas whenever the muse struck. I would whip out that notebook in class, while standing in line at a restaurant, or any time I needed to capture an idea. I guarded that notebook with my life, too, because if I lost it, I would lose all my ideas.

I amassed dozens of these little notebooks, and believe it or not, I still have them.

As I grew older, pens and paper became less useful in the era of digital. I went through a phase where I carried a voice recorder in my pocket and used that to record ideas. That was kind of fun, but a little cumbersome.

These days, I use my phone. I use a note taking app such as Evernote or Microsoft One Note to thumb ideas quickly into my phone whenever they strike. I keep those in a special notebook that I look through whenever I need inspiration. I capture the ideas and throw them in this notebook. I don't organize the pages; it's one of the few things in my writing life where chaos can be helpful. Sometimes it's helpful to see random associations.

Over the years, I have collected tens of thousands of notes and ideas. I'm not kidding. My notebooks are huge.

However you want to do it, consider creating an idea log. If you have one, pay attention to how you are capturing your notes to ensure that they will be helpful to you later. The more specific you can be, the better.

Here are some characteristics of a good, accurately captured idea:

- Describes where you were when the idea happened, and the date.
- Describes the idea in the five senses. Don't just describe what you see; describe how you might write the idea into your novel. Trust me, when you're lacking inspiration, you will want something that's easy to port over to your work-in-progress.
- Photos, video, and audio of the experience (if possible).

I included a few examples from my idea log to show how I capture ideas.

Notes from a Night Club

· · ·

I don't go to night clubs and bars. But my cousin visited me one summer, and he does, so being a good host, I took him around town so he could have some fun. He danced and socialized while I sat against the wall, watching people. Here's a note from that night.

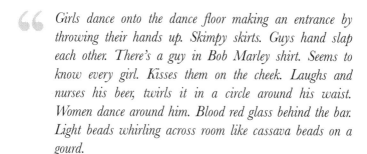

> *Girls dance onto the dance floor making an entrance by throwing their hands up. Skimpy skirts. Guys hand slap each other. There's a guy in Bob Marley shirt. Seems to know every girl. Kisses them on the cheek. Laughs and nurses his beer, twirls it in a circle around his waist. Women dance around him. Blood red glass behind the bar. Light beads whirling across room like cassava beads on a gourd.*

Regina

In this next example, my friend was telling me about a girl he just met. He was completely awestricken by her. To this day, I have never heard him gush about a woman like he did that night. Maybe that's why it stuck out to me. I captured our conversation (though I changed the woman's name and ethnicity).

> *Regina has cream-colored skin, like chai tea. Her skin matches her personality. Thick lips but not too thick, bluish-green eyes whose color you can't quite pin down—eyes that leave you dumbstruck in conversation when it's your time to speak. She likes to drink for the taste of alcohol—not for the drunkenness. She prefers gin to vodka, rum to whiskey. She adores flavored drinks and amarettos.*
>
> *She was born in Guyana. She's half-Lebanese and half-Chinese, and she went to school in Holland. She*

speaks English, Dutch, French, and German—maybe Farsi and Arabic too.

We were in a bookstore and I was looking at this art book. Oil paintings of Scottish castles.

"What are you reading?" she asked.

"An art book."

She snatched the book out of my hands and started thumbing through the pages. "I love art," she said.

I mentioned flamenco and her eyes grew wide—she was the only person on the trip who liked it.

Four Guys and a Little Girl

My wife and I used to live in an apartment complex. As with all apartment complexes, you never know who your neighbors are. There's always a constant stream of people moving in and out. One night, I had to run an errand and grab some dinner. It was a cool spring night. I encountered a group of people that I can still remember vividly so many years later.

Four guys in hoodies and baggy clothes approaching. Ominous. Little girl in a little checkered coat is between them. First guy in blue passes without a glance. Second guy in a bling hat says, "Hello."

I say, "How you doin'"

The little girl stares at me thoughtfully, and after a while says, "Daddy, you know everyone."

"No I don't," the guy in the bling hat says. "But I think it's nice to say hello to someone when they walk by."

"That's right," I say, nodding.

Another guy in the back of the group spits.

Bringing It All Together

． ． ．

I could list more examples, but I hope these are clear.

I also use my idea log for potential dialogue, catchy titles that I might use for novels and short stories, and other observations that defy categorization.

Keep an idea log. It's a daily action that will help you when you don't know what to write next.

Strategy #6: Take Naps

Naps are fun.

They serve the double purpose of rest and inspiration.

When your next story hits a snag, take a quick 15- to 20-minute nap. You'll wake up refreshed and ready to tackle the story again.

Personally, if I had the space in my office, I would put a couch there so I could take small naps during the day as needed.

Sleeping works because it gives your subconscious time to untangle any knots that are in your story. Sometimes distance and perspective is the best solution to the problem you're having in your story, and 15 to 20 minutes is sometimes all the subconscious needs.

So take naps.

They're good for you, and good for your subconscious.

Strategy #7: Track Your Daily Word Count and Set a Daily Range

You're probably wondering what tracking your daily word count has to do with "writer's block."

The saying "What gets measured gets managed" is the reason.

If you don't track your word count, you won't know how you are performing. You'll only have a gut feeling of whether you had a good day.

When you track your word count, you can track your performance in real-time and over time.

That performance should serve as a barometer for how you are doing.

Many successful authors recommend having a quota. Personally, I think quotas are too strict and put undue pressure on you if you have a bad day. I don't like having to perform above or below such an arbitrary line.

What has worked for me instead is to set a quota range based on my historical word counts and current enthusiasm for the project.

For example, on a normal day, I usually write between 2,500 and 5,000 words. That's somewhere between 17,500 and

35,000 words per week. Some weeks I am high, some weeks I am low, some weeks I'm well above the range, some weeks I'm well below the range.

A range makes me more comfortable because it's flexible. It suits my lifestyle better, accounting for the fact that not every day in my life is going to be the same. With a range, I can write comfortably knowing that as long as I am within the range, I have nothing to worry about.

I *do* worry, though, in two situations.

The first cause for alarm is when I fall below the range for more than two days at a time. I try to evaluate what caused it. This happens from time to time and usually resolves itself with minimal intervention as long as I keep writing.

The second cause for alarm is when I rise above my range for more than a week at a time. You're probably thinking, "Why worry? That's amazing!"

Here's why: this is just my personal experience and it may not affect you, but I have found that my biggest crashes always occur after I have an amazing run above my range. The euphoric high is almost always followed by a bone-crushing low.

I once wrote a full-length novel in 6 days. It was one of those rare novels where I literally hit *no* rough patches.

After finishing the novel, my next one was *hard.* I spent two weeks well below my range before I could gain momentum. All in all, everything averaged out for the month range-wise, but I learned from that experience and was ready for it the next time around, several books later, when I started flying through another novel.

I've learned to enjoy the highs and weather the lows. Again, this is just my personal experience, but I think it's helpful to share it with you so that you can be aware of your own quirks.

Strategy #8: Use Yesterday as a Baseline

You now know why a daily average is important.

Here's another mental tactic that I do every day: I use yesterday as a baseline.

If I have a really good day and write within my range, I think about the day ahead and figure out what it will take to perform at the same level. If I see roadblocks or things that might stop me from making the same progress tomorrow, I might try to write a few hundred more words today to try to offset the potential decrease. When tomorrow hits, I'll be more mindful of my potential handicap. Sometimes I can't do anything about it, and that's okay. At least I know in advance.

If I have a terrible day today and write below my range, I'll figure out how I can write within my range tomorrow. I usually tell myself something like "it can't get worse than today hopefully."

Another similar tactic that helps here is to have what I call a horizon.

I create deadlines for my novels. I write the deadline on a whiteboard next to my desk. Then I ignore the deadline. More often than not, I beat my deadlines by a few days.

Here's how I do it.

I visualize my project in terms of word count, but I only limit my vision to what I can see two days from now. That's my "horizon." I don't let myself think past that two days. No story, no character arcs beyond that point. I keep a narrow focus on only what I will finish in the next two days.

So, for example, let's say I'm 30,000 words into a 50,000-word book.

Let's pretend I had a good day within my range yesterday (let's say 3,500 words), and I want to have another day like yesterday today.

Doing that will put me at 33,500 at the end of the day today and 37,000 at the end of tomorrow.

Tomorrow is my horizon.

I've found that I write better when I live in the present. If I think about the ending when I'm writing the middle, that paralyzes me and introduces fear. I enjoy the writing process better too; since I don't outline, I like to be surprised at what happens in my stories as I write them. Aiming for yesterday's baseline and capping my thinking at tomorrow helps me do this.

Strategy #9: Look Backward (and Forward)

Call me sentimental, but I enjoy looking back at what I've done. I've written a lot of books, and it's great to take a minute and reflect on my progress every now and then.

Consider these tactics and do them regularly to stroke your ego, but be careful not to get lost in your glory days.

Where Were You a Week Ago? Month? Year? Two Years?

I do this once a month or as needed.

I ask myself, "Where was I a week ago?"

I think back to what I was working on last week. Usually, I've made good progress since then, and I can feel good about where I am.

I think back to what I was working on last month.

Then I think back to what I was working on the last year. And two years ago.

Then, I visualize ahead to the next week, keeping in mind my horizon. I do this just to build some momentum.

I jump ahead to the next month, year, and two years, visualizing myself writing all kinds of new stories and characters.

This tactic helps because it grounds you in the moment while also connecting you to the past and future.

For example, here's my visual at the time of writing this chapter.

January 28, 2018

> This week: I'm working on Be a Writing Machine. I'm about 14,000 words in.
>
> Last week: I finished the final chapter in Evil Waking, Book 3 of my Magic Trackers urban fantasy series.
>
> Last month (December 2017): I was hard at work, finishing Nightmare Stalkers, Book 2 in the Magic Trackers series.
>
> Last year (January 2017): I was just finishing Honor's Reserve, Book 1 in my Galaxy Mavericks space opera series, the first of 9 books. Good times.
>
> Two years ago (January 2016): I was barely starting Old Dark, Book 1 in The Last Dragon Lord dark fantasy series. I really struggled to get this book going, and I remember languishing in the first act, unsure if I'd ever finish it. Seriously, it was a crisis. (And look at me now!)
>
> Next week: I'm moving really fast through Be a Writing Machine and will probably be done with it. At this point, I'll be working on the cover and getting the book off to my editor.

Next month: I'll be deep into Book 1 of my next
series, a post-apocalyptic thriller. Can't wait
to start it.

Next year (January 2019): I'll be done with my
post-apocalyptic series. My next series will
likely be steampunk. If I haven't started it
already, I'll be starting it soon.

Two years from now (January 2020): Hell if I
know! But I'll be celebrating the 60-book
mark by now, and that's something to be
excited about.

Visualization is a powerful technique that will serve as
rocket fuel to your subconscious. Don't neglect it.

Mark the Anniversaries of Your Books

I have a Google calendar titled "Book Anniversaries." I have
entered the publication date of all my books, and I have it set
so that I receive an email notification at 5AM on the anniver-
sary of the book's birthday.

Getting those notifications when I wake up is a fun way to
start my day. I often forget when the anniversaries are, so it's
always a pleasant surprise.

Mark the Time Other Ways

For example, I go to the dentist twice a year, usually in January
and in June.

When I'm sitting in the chair getting my teeth cleaned, it's a good time to think about what book I'm on now compared to my last visit, and where I think I'll be at the next visit.

It's simple but fun.

Strategy #10: Take Care of Yourself

Eat right.

Exercise.

Get a full night's sleep.

I shouldn't have to tell you this, but I do. Hell, I *try* to do these things, but I don't always succeed.

I drink a lot of loose leaf tea. I find that drinking it helps with my mood and it keeps me mellow.

Many writers like coffee, the patron saint of the scribe. If that works for you, cool.

I also go on daily walks, which is something a lot of people do. It works.

Just remember to take care of yourself. You can't be prolific if you're dead at a young age!

Strategy #11: Know When to Go Nuclear

This one's controversial, but it works.

Before we continue, I want you to identify the areas of a novel when you generally hit rough patches.

It could be the beginning, middle, end. Pick the one that gives you the most trouble.

Then, when you hit that section in your next work in progress, go nuclear.

Drop off the grid and don't communicate with friends and family. Let only your closest loved ones know where and when to find you.

Don't check Facebook. Don't watch Netflix. Don't go out to clubs, or the bar, or whatever you like to do. Don't do it.

Write the hell out of the section of the novel that gives you trouble. Don't lift your head up until you're done.

This might take you a few hours. It could take you a few days.

But when you're done, you'll be able to rest knowing that you're finished with the toughest part of your novel.

Again, this is controversial. I'm telling you to be antisocial...

But look at it this way: you know that this section of the novel is your historical weakness. You know that if you *don't* do something about it, you could lose your momentum. Right? Right?

If you want to be prolific, you have to care about getting things done. Sometimes you have to make some sacrifices to get there.

To quote that age-old philosopher, Tommy Pickles: a baby's gotta do what a baby's gotta do.

I don't recommend that you *always* go nuclear. That's destructive to both yourself and your family. But some projects will require it. You'll know which ones they are.

Don't worry about your friends and family. Communicate with them about when you're going to go nuclear and how long you think it will take. If they love you, they'll understand. They'll be there for you when you're done. Just make sure you give them the time and love that *they* need once you reach your goal.

Writer's Block Part 3:
Strategies to Combat
Lack of Inspiration

Until now we've been talking about general maintenance strategies to keep you motivated. Those were all-season strategies that you can use in virtually any situation.

But what if those strategies don't work?

What if you identify that your "writer's block" stems from lack of inspiration?

Try the strategies in this section.

Strategy #1: Drift Until You
Find Your Way

It happens to all of us: you're in the middle of your work in progress, and you have no idea what to do next.

You try all of the general strategies, but you can't get motivated.

You listen to your subconscious, but it's surprisingly silent.

Sometimes it's okay to stop writing.

There, I said it.

Let me say it again: sometimes it's okay to stop writing.

Your subconscious occasionally needs time and distance to untangle your story. And sometimes that means that you need to step away from your story.

When this happens, I need to step away from the story and "drift," which is my way of floating through life, looking for a trigger or an inspiration that will move the story forward. When I drift, I'm on high alert. I'm extremely introspective, sensitive, and sometimes moody. That's because I'm looking for the smallest sign I can find for inspiration. When I find it, life is good.

Recently, I let myself drift while working on my *Galaxy Mavericks* series. I was between Books 7 and 8, which is a major spot in the story where everything changes and the series adopts a slightly different tone. I knew how I wanted to proceed and I knew exactly where I wanted Book 8 to start, but I wasn't feeling motivated. I listened to myself and couldn't figure out why. I just couldn't start the book.

I put the book aside, focusing instead on putting extra hours into my day job. This lasted for about a day. Then, on a Friday night, my wife and I spontaneously went to a home and garden show at a local convention center.

The sights and the smells!

I remember the event vividly. And I remember being inspired, not by anything in particular, but just by being there. I spotted a person who made a good basis for a minor character that I wanted to introduce late in the series, but nothing major.

When I got home that night, I started writing as if I had never had a problem. The experience at the home and garden show was a contact high for me, and it was what my subconscious needed to get motivated.

Drifting can be powerful, but don't procrastinate. That's different.

Drifting requires you to be on a constant lookout. It's passive but in the best possible way. Writing is always on the top of your mind. Procrastination is the opposite; it's lazy and you're usually doing anything to avoid writing. If you find yourself procrastinating whenever you try to drift, then this strategy is not for you.

This strategy is for writers who have enough self-discipline to force themselves into the chair and write again if drifting doesn't find them inspiration after, say, a day or so.

Strategy #2: Put Your Project Away

Are you working on the right project?

If not, that could be driving your lack of inspiration.

This is another strategy that is not for the faint of heart.

It requires you to quit working on your work in progress. Pack it up and put it away. Then go work on something else.

As I like to say, sometimes a project can benefit from time and distance. If you can't get excited about what you're working on, you're working on the wrong thing.

I've abandoned a fair number of projects over the years, mostly nonfiction. I start off writing it thinking that it will be a good fit, but about halfway through, I realize that it's not. As soon as I discover this, I ditch the project immediately.

I've ditched novels too.

Think about what motivates you. Are you getting that in your current project? If so, continue. If not, think twice about it.

Life is short. Spend it working only on the projects that inspire you.

Strategy #3: Backtrack and Change Direction in Your Story

Lack of inspiration can also strike when you've gone astray in your story.

This happens to me a lot.

Sometimes, I write past where I need to be. It requires me to backtrack to the spot where things went wrong, delete everything after, and charge forward.

I've never backtracked more than a thousand words or so, but I suppose an amount higher than that could happen.

The key to avoid having to ever use this strategy is to listen to your subconscious and don't deviate from it.

Just know that backtracking can be a helpful strategy every now and again if you ever find yourself in a bad way.

Don't feel bad about deleting words. I know it can be painful, but words are just words. Everything you do should be in service of your story and your readers. Remember to be attached and unattached at the same time.

But if you find yourself deleting thousands upon thousands of words, you have another problem entirely. It means you're not listening to yourself.

Strategy #4: The Power of Switching

If you can't write forward, think about switching: switching projects, switching locales in which you write, switching the way that you write, etc.

Switching is powerful in many ways.

First, it introduces new experiences to your subconscious, which can help you break past a blockage.

Second, it may be what you need.

Switching Projects

Early on in my writing career, I liked to have two projects going at the same time. Project A was my primary focus. Project B was a side project that I worked on occasionally if I hit a roadblock in Project A.

That worked pretty well for me.

These days, I write so fast that I don't need to switch between projects, but this could be a helpful strategy for you.

. . .

Switching Locales

If you're struggling while writing in your home office, take your computer and go to the coffee shop for a couple hours. If you normally write in coffee shops, go to a library and rent a conference room. Sometimes writing in a new place is all the inspiration you need to keep going.

Switching Your Writing Style

If you write on your laptop primarily, try writing on your phone.

If you write on your phone primarily, try writing on your desktop.

Hell, try writing a chapter by hand.

Even better, try dictation.

Switching up your style when you're blocked can be helpful because it requires you to think in a different way and engages different parts of your brain.

I mentioned causally earlier that I struggled with the first act of *Old Dark*. At this point, I hadn't adopted writing on my phone yet, and I could not get motivated to even start the novel.

After a week of struggling, I switched to dictation. Through dictating the novel, I discovered that I wasn't getting the character's voices right. Dictation solved that problem real quick.

Strategy #5: Go on a Date (with Yourself)

When the words won't flow, sometimes you need to do something totally different, something totally outside of your comfort zone.

Go on a date with yourself.

Go to a local tea tasting.

Learn how to build a bookcase.

Attend a local beer festival.

Learn how to salsa dance.

Visit a different kind of retail shop. Never quilted in your life? Cool. Go to a quilt shop just to see what it's like.

Going on dates with yourself regularly is good auto to prevent lack of inspiration, but it's also a good way to combat lack of inspiration when the words aren't flowing like usual.

The dates don't have to be elaborate. They just have to put you outside of your comfort zone for a little while.

Strategy #6: Microfocus

When the words won't flow, it can be agonizing. You don't know what to do, and you don't have the inspiration.

When the other strategies aren't working, and you're losing hope, try this one.

It's called micro focusing.

You visualize the spot in the story where you are stuck, and you focus on the next sentence.

Literally. The next sentence.

Don't focus on the story. Don't focus on the character. Just focus on the next sentence.

Write it and don't think about it.

Then write the next sentence.

I make this sound easy, but trust me, when you're in the moment, it's really hard. In fact, it's so hard that you'll often wonder how you'll ever finish the novel. Trust me, I get it.

When you're not inspired, sometimes you have to sit in the chair and get work done. It's hard, but there's no way around it, unfortunately.

The key here is to put your butt in the chair and don't let

yourself get up until you write a substantial amount. That's the hard part.

This is also a strategy you can use to combat fear.

Strategy #7: Visualize Yourself
Untangling the Problem

This strategy is simple.

If you ever lack inspiration, just visualize yourself untangling the problem.

Here's what I do.

When I'm meditating, I visualize my story, and I imagine all the scenes and characters twisted into a nasty knot. I visualize my hands around the knot, slowly untying it until everything is resolved.

Sometimes that doesn't work, so then I imagine that the knot is the Gordian knot and I cut the damn thing with an imaginary sword. Works every time.

Strategy #8: Outline (in Your Mind)

Yes, yes, I've told you *not* to outline.

But when you're stuck and don't have inspiration, sometimes outlining can be helpful.

Here's what I do.

Let's say I'm writing a story where I know Point A and say, Point F, but everything in between is a mystery and I can't see it. This happens to me all the time; I can see parts of the story, but there are gaps in between.

If I am not enjoying this section of the book, I'll break my "horizon" rule and *think* about what could potentially happen between Point A and Point F.

I *think* about it, but I don't write it down.

Point B is this; Point C is maybe that; Point D could possibly be this, and so on.

I allow my subconscious to do this, not my inner critic.

I keep this mental outline in my mind, and I let it float there, fully knowing that it could change.

Then I estimate the potential word counts for each point. I compare that to where I am in the book currently. That allows me to map out when I will potentially be finished with the rough patch.

I *never, ever* write the outline down. That would invite the inner critic to start playing with it. I don't want that.

By keeping the outline in my mind, my subconscious can play with it uninterrupted.

This is different from traditional outlining because I'm outlining in the moment and only as needed. Once I'm done with the outline, I forget that I ever did it.

This is the only time I recommend outlining *prior* to writing.

Strategy #9: Listen To Music While You Write

Music can help you through almost any rough patch.

Everyone has different interests, so I won't recommend any music, as much as I would love to.

Personally, I'm a big fan of video game music. I'm somewhat of a connoisseur, and I own hundreds of albums. Video game music is fantastic with conveying moods and emotions, and I have playlists for virtually every kind of mood and situation. Battles. Introspection. Climaxes. Sadness.

What has worked for me is to create playlists for the book I'm writing with music that best matches the mood. Then I listen to that playlist over and over. And over. And over. I pretend that the music is part of the story I'm writing.

When I'm stuck, I try to find additional songs I can add to the book's playlist.

What you do with your music is up to you. Just know that it can help you power through a rough patch.

I suspect, though, that most people reading this have no issues getting inspired by music. Just a hunch.

Writer's Block Part 4:
Strategies to
Combat Fear

I can't overstate enough that fear is ever-shifting and relentless.

We all have fear. It lives with us when we write, and it's just a matter of time before it tries to stop you.

If there's one thing I can teach you about how I've dealt with my struggles, it's that everything you want in life is on the other side of fear. Most people don't ever get to the other side.

But there's a misconception about fear that I want to dispel, and that's the myth that you can *overcome* fear.

That's not true.

At least, it's not true for me.

Fear cannot be overcome. It *can*, however, be minimized and dealt with. Those are the only solutions you can hope and pray for.

If you can't overcome fear, then that means you have to live with it. You have to treat it like you do a snoopy neighbor. You can ignore them all you want, but it's just a matter of time before you have to deal with them in some form.

If you know that and accept it, you've won half the battle. Seriously.

The other half of the battle is learning the strategies in this section to arm yourself against fear's devilish tactics.

Fear will confuse you, sabotage you, sadden you, and make you hate yourself, to say the least.

The best way to fight fear is with the right mindset. The strategies in this section work, but they are much more effective if you're in the right mindset.

Even if you are in the right mindset, I unfortunately have to tell you that there will be many times where you will face a fear without a go-to strategy you can use. So you must learn to fight it with every square inch of your body and soul.

You have to understand that you are up against a foe who wants nothing but your very destruction.

Don't believe anything it says and don't ever doubt yourself.

Strategy #1: Isolate Your Fears

In order to fight fear, you have to know where it's coming from. Otherwise, you may not employ the right strategy against it.

To recap, here are some of the major fears that I have faced throughout my career.

This is not an exhaustive list by any means.

Fear of Inadequacy

Also known as inferiority complex.

This fear makes you believe that you're not worthy enough, that you don't have what it takes to survive in the writing game.

For me, my fear of inadequacy stems from my father's abandonment, childhood bullying, and my race and the way I've been treated because of it.

Of course I'm more than adequate, but it doesn't always feel that way.

On days when this fear shows up, nothing I do ever seems

to be good enough. I compare myself to others and feel like I can't measure up.

This fear is scary deadly because it rewires your mind. I've had days where I feel super inadequate, and *nothing* can change my mind. Then, the next day, when the fear disappears, I'll dismiss everything I felt yesterday because I realize what a terrible hold it had over me.

This is one of the worst fears that I have to deal with, and it visits me fairly often. The general maintenance strategies I follow in this book often help to ensure that this fear only lingers for a day or so. But I've been a victim of this fear for weeks at a time and it's agonizing. I don't wish it on even the biggest douchebag writers.

When general maintenance strategies don't work, the only way I have found to kill this fear is to recognize when I'm being irrational. The moment I do, I stop writing for the day, or I aim for half of my normal range. I watch inspirational YouTube videos, do things to take my mind off writing, and ignore the fear as much as I can.

Pro tip about fear: it's like the weather. It comes in waves. Much like a summer thunderstorm that spawns seemingly out of nowhere and vanishes as quickly as it came, so does fear.

With the fear of inadequacy, I pop up my mental umbrella and wait it out.

Fear of Rejection

This is my least favorite fear. (Is it possible to have a favorite fear?)

Fear of rejection hurts me pretty badly because I've been rejected in some way or form my whole life.

I've been rejected because I am black. I won't go into that here.

I've been rejected by my father.

I've been rejected by friends. Family. Coworkers.

Something about this fear hits me deep down, probably more than most.

That's why I avoid anything in publishing where rejection is a component, whenever possible. It's why I gave up on traditional publishing early. I didn't feel like sitting around waiting for people to reject me. That's crazy!

It's also why I don't enjoy submitting short stories and poems to magazines. I know that it's an important way to gain new readers, but I don't do well with the rejection. I once sent a poem out to 100 different magazines, one at a time, over the course of a year, only to get rejected 100 times. I did this again with 26 more poems, and each one was rejected.

I like to pretend that I don't care, but I do. It screws with my mind too much.

Trust me when I say I have a thick skin, but something about the submission process doesn't sit well with my spirit. So I don't do it if I don't have to. Personal choice. Doesn't mean you shouldn't, but I'm simply sharing how I manage this fear.

Of course, there is the fear of being rejected by readers, which happens for me more often than it does not. I have learned to cope with this by publishing on my own terms.

It's why I write entire series at a time before launching them, for example. I do this, one, because I write fast enough to do it, and two, if the series fails, it's okay because I'm already in the land of the next story and don't have to worry about dwelling on the failure. Again, this is highly personal and specific to me, but publishing on my own terms is how I deal with a fear that otherwise would singlehandedly limit my writing output.

.   .   .

Fear of Abandonment

Similar to the fear of rejection, the fear of abandonment differs when I'm experiencing success.

Maybe Book 1 in my new series is doing really well, but what if readers actually hate Book 1 and don't buy the rest of the books in the series?

The only way to fight this one is to not check your sales so often.

Fear of Dying

Yes, I worry about dying.

I worry that I'll die before experiencing success. It's perfectly human.

The way to fight this one is to use this fear against itself.

Paranoia can be a good thing, especially when you use it to charge forward in your story.

Diagnosing Your Fear

Now that I've shared some of my biggest fears with you (I feel naked and vulnerable now!), let me tell you how I diagnose my fears.

First, I determine where the fear is coming from. This is key.

Is it coming from the story?

Is it coming from what I think will be the finished product?

Is it coming from somewhere else other than the writing?

If it's the story, I can usually tell because the story will be on my mind more often than usual.

If it's the finished product, I can tell because I find myself thinking ahead to sales and what readers will think.

If it's an external fear, that's usually obvious too if something is going on at work, such as the rumor of layoffs or the loss of an important client.

Diagnosing the fear is the most important step because once you do that, you can learn how to fight it more effectively.

Strategy #2: Follow Your Fingers

Sometimes you just have to follow your fingers.

Fear will show up and try to persuade you that you're terrible.

Sometimes you won't be able to diminish its evil voice. You won't know what to do.

It'll be eight o'clock in the morning and you'll despair because you've only written 200 words for the day and have so much farther to go.

The way forward is to follow your fingers.

Just type the next word and listen to your subconscious the best you can. Trust yourself to keep taking the next step even if fear tries to stop you.

Follow your fingers. They will help you escape from the fear.

Strategy #3: Write Around the Fear

If you find yourself staring in the face of fear, unable to move forward, try this strategy.

Do you write your novels in linear fashion?

Have you ever considered doing it another way?

If you're a plotter, this won't work for you.

Pantsers, pay attention because this will help you.

Let's say you're in the fifth chapter of what will probably be a 30-chapter book.

What if you jumped to Chapter 20 and wrote backwards?

Or what if you wrote Chapter 20, then 24, then 34, then back to Chapter 6?

It sounds strange, but I've written novels backward and out of order before. I've written entire *series* backwards.

Why does this work as a strategy against fear?

Because it confuses it.

When you leapfrog fear and then approach it from the rear, you can defeat it by sheer virtue of your boldness.

This strategy also works because fear may only inhabit certain parts of your work in progress. If you jump ahead to parts where it does not reside, you will boost your confidence and you'll therefore be able to fight it more effectively.

However, the only downside to this strategy is that it can backfire on you. Don't do it if you're dealing with fear of inadequacy or something similar. Otherwise, you'll paralyze yourself even further.

This strategy is advanced and not for everyone, but it does work.

Strategy #4: Make Meaningful Connections

You can't fight fear alone.

If you can't deal with it, consider getting some help.

Hang out with a friend. Call an old buddy you haven't talked to in a while.

Sometimes you need camaraderie in order to steel yourself against your opponent. God knows I do.

Note that this is, in many ways, the opposite of what I recommended when you lack inspiration.

When you lack inspiration, you need time with yourself (usually). When you're suffering from fear, you need time away from yourself.

This works great when you're feeling inadequate too because nothing builds you up like a true friend.

Strategy #5: Think Ahead

Another way to fight fear is to be smarter than it and think ahead. Visualize yourself shoving the fear aside and finishing your manuscript.

Also, consider repeating the following affirmations to yourself:

When this book is done and readers are reading it, they won't even notice that I struggled in Chapter 12.

When I look back on this book two years from now, I'm not even going to remember where I struggled.

Nothing will stop me from getting this book into my readers' hands.

Remember, everything you want is on the other side of fear.

Visualize yourself on the other side.

These affirmations do just that. In order for them to be true, you will have had to beat the fear back. Fear doesn't like that. It doesn't like you thinking outside of the present.

Beat it at its own game and focus on the future.

Create affirmations and positive thoughts of your own based on the problem you're having. You'll find that it helps you stay focused on the task at hand.

Strategy #6: Freewrite

This strategy is my favorite way to combat fear.

Freewriting is a writing session where you write whatever comes to your mind for a set period of time, say 5 or 10 minutes.

The nice part about freewriting is that you can use it to write about the very fear you're facing.

Write and write and write until your timer goes off. Don't hit the return key.

When you're done, don't read what you wrote. Throw it away, take a quick walk, drink tea, or have meditation break. Then start again on your story.

It's amazing how well this works.

Freewriting is useful in other ways too. Some people use it to get inside the head of their characters. Others use it to clear out their minds prior to writing—an active meditation of the hands, if you will.

Personally, I find freewriting to be most helpful in fighting fear. I don't find it to helpful in finding inspiration, but that's just me.

I went through a period where I freewrote every day. I don't recommend that. Otherwise, it will become a crutch. Use it only as needed.

Next Steps

You made it!

I'm glad you made it this far. I hope this book gave you some inspiration on how to shape your writing career. My deepest hope and prayer is that you found *something* useful within these pages.

As I said in the intro chapter, I wrote this book because of a spiritual promise I made to myself. Sure, sales are nice, but that is the least of my concerns. And no, I'm not selling you a $1,000 course or asking you to sign up for a newsletter. Seriously. All I care about is whether I made a difference in someone's life.

I have a skill that is unusual—writing really fast—and my goal with this book was to teach others how to do it.

So thanks for sticking with me.

For next steps, I want you to do two things.

First, I want you to remember the areas you need to focus on:

- Mindset
- Mastering your tools

- Time management
- Writing smarter
- General maintenance strategies to keep you motivated
- Combating lack of inspiration
- Combating of fear

Those are the competencies you need to work on. Master them, and you'll amaze yourself at how prolific you will become in a short amount of time.

Second, I'd like to recommend you the following books:

- *Writing into the Dark* by Dean Wesley Smith
- *Techniques of the Selling Writer* by Dwight V. Swain
- *Active Setting Series* by Mary Buckham
- *The Pursuit of Perfection* by Kristine Kathryn Rusch
- *How to Write Pulp Fiction* by James Scott Bell
- *Become an Idea Machine* by Claudia Azula Altucher
- *Writer Better, Faster* by Monica Leonelle
- *The Writer's Guide to Training Your Dragon* by Scott Baker
- *Be the Gateway: A Practical Guide to Sharing Your Creative Work and Engaging An Audience* by Dan Blank

Each of these books tackles one of the core competencies above. They will also help you hone your craft. If you want to check them out, I've compiled a (US only) Amazon shopping list where you can grab them conveniently. Find it at www.michaellaronn.com/writingmachinebooks.

This is an affiliate link, and I do receive a small commission if you buy from this link (doesn't cost you a thing). If you found this book helpful, consider helping a brother out.

I also have a YouTube channel called Author Level Up. I publish videos there that will help you write better, be a better

authorpreneur, and market your books: <u>www.</u>
<u>authorlevelup.com</u>.

I wish you all the best in your writing career. I hope you are able to write faster so you can tell all the stories in your head. I hope to see you on the list of most prolific authors ever! I know that I'll be trying to hit that list!

I've taught you everything I know.

Now go write.

Peace, love, and light,
    M.L. Ronn

Read Next: Mental Models for Writers

Here's an excerpt from the next book in this series, *Mental Models for Writers: 73 Ways to Elevate Your Thinking, Improve Your Writing, and Capture Success.*

———

"Mike, hand me the Allen wrench."

An insistent hand waved and got my attention as I stood at the foot of a bed that my grandfather and I were putting together. My grandfather was under the bed, straining to get the right angle for a corner screw.

I was six years old at the time and had no clue what an Allen wrench was. I was admiring the Michael Jordan poster above my wall that I had received from my birthday along with this bed, the limited edition one where he's making one of the most famous slam dunks of all time. I imagined the journalists' photoflashes blinking and the crowd gasping in anticipation, just before he slammed the ball in the net…

"Mike. The Allen wrench."

My grandfather's gravelly voice pulled me from my thoughts. I looked down at his cluttered toolbox and anxiety overcame me. Was it the crescent-looking thing that I thought I saw Super Mario use once? Which size?

I handed my grandfather tool after tool—crescent wrench, flathead screwdriver, needle-nosed pliers—but to no avail. Eventually, he rolled from under the bed, seized the little Allen wrench sitting directly in front of my face, and went back to work.

I wasn't much help to my grandfather that day. He put the bed together effortlessly, as he always did with household projects. As I grew older, his "handiness" was lost on me. Hey, I'm a writer. What would you expect?

But one piece of advice he gave always stuck with me: there's a tool for every job, and finding it is half the work.

Even though I never learned to be handy myself, I always admired handy people and how they were able to master the various skillsets that were needed for virtually any job. No matter what project they faced, they always knew the right tools and what steps to follow, and whenever problems came up, they solved them easily.

When I became a writer, I was astonished to discover that the only real tool you needed was a writing app, and that there is a shocking level of non-uniformity about how writers do things. Unlike installing a toilet, which has several key steps, structure doesn't exist in the writing world.

How do you write a novel? Ask a million writers, you'll get a million different answers.

How do you decide what book to write?

How do you open a chapter?

How do you make readers care about a character?

The fact that there is no uniformity is one of our greatest advantages—each of us can find our own way and live our careers however we want. But if you're anything like me and want to try and make sense of the world around you and want a little structure, how do you do it?

The result is that we stumble our way through the writing life, with no real rhyme or reason about how or why we do things. When we achieve success, and people ask us how we became successful, we give answers like "work really hard," "or just keep writing," or "write crappy first drafts."

Outside of writing apps and books, there are few physical tools to help us navigate the writing life. The tools we writers need to build careers in today's world of publishing are 99 percent mental. Mental models, to be precise.

Mental Models Represent How We Think

Put simply, a mental model is a framework of thinking to help you solve a particular problem. It's the equivalent of using a miter saw to cut crown molding trim or an angled paint brush to paint corners. They make the job so much easier.

With a mental model, you get a mode of attack that helps you grapple with a problem and ultimately beat it. Mental models have been used for centuries in just about every field other than writing. For example, take one of the most common models, Hanlon's Razor, which is best described as "never ascribe to malice which is adequately explained by stupidity."

The model assumes that most people in life aren't out to get you. That coworker who didn't send you the final copy of your group presentation ahead of the meeting with your boss? Maybe he wasn't trying to sabotage you. Maybe he just forgot, or he got sidetracked by someone stopping by his desk to chat. Or maybe he waited until the last minute to put his changes on the presentation. In any case, there are at least a dozen different reasons why he might have sent you the email late rather than assuming he hates you. Therefore, when you're facing a problem with another person and the first thing you think of is sabotage, remembering Hanlon's Razor can help you avoid a blind spot by assuming incompetence rather than malice. Instead of being angry, you can instead remain calm and ask questions that will help you figure out the root cause of the other person's problem and how you can solve it. From that exchange comes progress rather than tension. The true benefit of Hanlon's Razor is that nine times out of ten, people's actions do truly stem from incompetence, not malice.

That's how mental models are designed to work. They eliminate blind spots and elevate your thinking.

If we were to apply Hanlon's Razor to the writing life, it would give us insights into the ways that other authors, service providers, and book retailers operate, and it would give us some guidance in how to deal with issues as they come up. Maybe the person copying the first line of your book description doesn't understand that what they're doing is ethically wrong, for example.

Let's use another example. Take Sir Isaac Newton's first law, the law of inertia, which says that an object at rest will remain at rest until acted upon by an unbalanced force. If you're a nonfiction writer wanting to convince people to lose weight, apply the law of inertia to your thinking and you immediately understand that a person who doesn't work out and eat right won't start working out and eating right unless something big happens in their life to make them change their habits—i.e. a heart attack or a health scare. So to use the mental model properly, you might start thinking of ways that YOU could be the unbalanced force that Newton writes about. What would it take to make a real, lasting difference in your readers' lives?

If you still need convincing about why mental models are useful, consider that Charlie Munger is one of their most popular proponents. Don't know the name? He's the second-in-command to Warren Buffet at Berkshire Hathaway—you know, *that Warren Buffet,* one of the richest men in the world. Munger used mental models to help him make smart investments and build Berkshire Hathaway into the financial juggernaut that it is today. If you look at Berkshire's portfolio, many of the companies they invest in don't immediately make sense. Low-cost insurance companies, utility companies, furniture stores…huh?

But Buffet and Munger have different North Stars than you and I. They found opportunities in unusual places and solved problems in ways that grace the pages of business textbooks today, all because of their adoption of mental models.

Munger talked about drawing upon a "latticework of models" to solve problems. You start by collecting a lot of different models—many from fields other than yours, like science, engineering, mathematics, etc.—and when you need to make a decision, you cycle through the models in your head to see which one helps you best address the issue at hand. The act of transporting a model from one field to another is what mental model expert James Clear calls "liquid knowledge."

Clear writes, "World-class thinkers are often silo-free thinkers. They avoid looking at life through the lens of one subject. Instead, they develop 'liquid knowledge' that flows easily from one topic to the next."

I don't know about you, but if mental models are good enough for Charlie Munger and Warren Buffet, they're good enough for me.

Writing is Really Just Problem-Solving in Disguise

Consider this. According to Tom Vanderbilt, author of the book *Traffic: Why We Drive the Way We Do (And What It Says About Us)*, a driver makes a decision every 100 feet on average.

If I want to drive to the grocery store that's one mile away from my house, that means I have to make 52.8 decisions on the way there. This includes whether to go right or left out of my subdivision (both will get me there), whether to slow down for the family of deer on the side of the road, if I should let the little girl on a tricycle cross ahead of me before pulling forward at a stop sign, even though I have the right of way, if I should change lanes or wait for the pickup truck tailgating me to pass, if I should stop at the yellow light or stomp on the accelerator, and last but not least, where the heck to park in the grocery store lot.

Traffic is a phenomenal book, and I suggest you check it out. But let's liquify Vanderbilt's idea and apply it to writing. **What if it were true that writers had to make decisions every 100 words in their manuscripts?**

Think about the book you're writing right now. Think about the last writing session you had. It was smooth and effortless, right??

Probably not. You probably had to make some tough decisions about your characters, your setting, your dialogue, and even the sentences and words you used. What if mental models could help you in your everyday writing sessions?

What if mental models could help you at *every juncture* in the writing life?

That's why I wrote this book.

When I think about my writing life over the last five years since I became a professional writer, I think of the problems that I had to solve—writing that first draft, editing that draft into oblivion, learning how to format my book, publish my book, and so on. I think about my first Amazon Advertising ads being failures and the struggles I overcame to make them profitable. And most importantly, I think about the problems in my manuscripts that popped up that seemed insurmountable at the time—plot holes, logistics of getting the hero from point A to point B, and simple yet important things like how a character can take a fire extinguisher out of a glass panel without a key—and how I always found a way around them.

That's why I believe that writing is really just problem-solving in disguise. Learn how to become a really good problem solver, and there's no obstacle in the world of writing that you can't barrel through, especially when you're stuck in the murky middle of your manuscript.

Why I'm Qualified to Write a Book About Mental Models

. . .

Let's get a couple things out of the way. First, I'm not a psychologist, sociologist, or philosopher—you know, the type that you'd expect to be talking about this stuff.

I don't have a Ph.D., unless you count the honorary one I got from the school of hard knocks.

I haven't done shrewd scientific research or conducted rigorous sociological experiments about the nature of the human brain when it uses mental models.

I'm just a writer who lives in Iowa. A science fiction and fantasy writer, at that.

But here's what I do have: practical experience.

To date, I have written over 50 books, all while working as a manager at a Fortune 100 insurance company, raising a family with a rambunctious toddler, attending law school in the evenings, teaching insurance classes, co-hosting two podcasts, running a weekly YouTube channel called Author Level Up for writers that's 13,000 subscribers and growing (at the time of this writing), and serving as a team member on The Alliance of Independent Authors, a nonprofit dedicated to promoting ethics and excellence in the self-publishing community. I've spoken to crowds of over 1,000 people about writing and time management, and my life is a crazy vortex most days.

So many people ask me how I find the time to do all the things I do on a regular basis.

I could take the easy way out and say "hard work," but really, it's because I learned to see past blind spots and see my world differently. I am able to accomplish so much so quickly because I've changed my thinking. I don't see problems as problems, but as opportunities. And opportunities excite me. Combine that with mental models, an analytical mind that loves to solve puzzles, and a monk-like dedication to the craft of writing, and you have a blueprint to my achievements.

I wouldn't be where I am today without mental models. I can teach you what I've learned. This book is my way of codifying the models I've used as a writer so that other writers can use them.

Many of the mental model books on the market today are written for general audiences, and while they're excellent books, they don't have examples specifically tailored for *writers*. They also focus primarily on theory.

Theory is great, but it's useless if you can't put it into practice.

One of my favorite online courses ever is *Video Foundations* with Anthony Q. Artis, which I took to learn the art of video editing for my YouTube videos. In that series, Artis, a seasoned video director, teaches you how to use video equipment like a professional. He talks about video theory and then shoots it down, opting for practicality above all things. One of my favorite quotes from him is "I'm not an academic. I'm a pracademic."

I, too, am a pracademic.

In this book, I'll cover some of the most popular mental models and I will make them practical and relate them to the writing life so you can start using them right away. But many of the models I cover can't be found anywhere else; they're liquid knowledge I learned as an employee in corporate America, as a writer muddling through a beginning career, as a student in law classes, and most importantly, as a mentee listening to wise mentors from virtually every area of my life.

Where the science is lacking, I've substituted my own practical experience. If you were looking for thoroughly-researched science and psychology, you won't find it here. Other mental model books on the market will be a better fit for you. But in these pages, you will find interesting stories that will challenge you to think differently.

This book is my vision of what it means to think, live, and prosper as a writer in the 21st century.

· · ·

Overview of This Book

If you're ready to elevate your thinking, improve your writing, and capture success in a different way, keep reading.

I've broken the book into several sections.

The **Creativity** section explores models you can use to boost your creativity and take your writing to new heights.

The **Problem-Solving and Decision-Making** section explores models that will help you solve virtually any problem you encounter in the writing life. It's the largest section in the book and vitally important.

The **Productivity** section will give you models to be more productive and help you get out of your own way.

The **Skills** section explores models that will help you master the skills that every writer needs to thrive in the future.

The **Fiction Writing** section contains models specifically tailored for fiction writing.

And finally, the **Marketing & Promotion** section provides some models to help you think about marketing differently.

I've also included an Appendix that gathers summaries of all the models in one place for your convenience when you're done reading, as well as links to all the resources I mention in the book.

You're moving into unexplored territory in the writing world, one that will yield untold treasures if you embrace it. You'll find the right tools for every job you can think of as a writer, and like my grandfather always said, that's half the work.

There's one thing I learned about being a writer that gets me excited every day, and it speaks to the true power we have: learn how to master physical tools, and you will build something that lasts for a century. But learn how to master your mind, and you will build something that lasts forever.

Onward, my pracademics, and let's have some fun.

———

Want to read more?

Grab your copy of *Mental Models for Writers* today. Available in ebook, paperback, and audiobook formats at your favorite retailer: www.authorlevelup.com/mentalmodels

Meet M.L. Ronn

Science fiction and fantasy on the wild side!

M.L. Ronn (Michael La Ronn) is the author of many science fiction and fantasy novels including *The Good Necromancer*, *Android X,* and *The Last Dragon Lord* series.

In 2012, a life-threatening illness made him realize that storytelling was his #1 passion. He's devoted his life to writing ever since, making up whatever story makes him fall out of his chair laughing the hardest. Every day.

Learn more about Michael
www.authorlevelup.com (for writers)
www.michaellaronn.com (fiction)

More Books by M.L. Ronn

Books for Writers

Indie Author Confidential (Series)
    How to Write Your First Novel
    Be a Writing Machine
    Mental Models for Writers
    The Indie Writer's Encyclopedia
    The Indie Author Atlas
    The Indie Author Bestiary
    The Reader's Bill of Rights
    The Self-Publishing Compendium
    150 Self-Publishing Questions Answered
    Authors, Steal This Book
    The Indie Author Strategy Guide
    How to Dictate a Book
    Advanced Author Editing
    Keep Your Books Selling
    The Author Estate Handbook
    The Author Heir Handbook

Interactive Fiction: How to Engage Readers and Push the Boundaries of Story Telling

Indie Poet Rock Star

Indie Poet Formatting

2016 Indie Author State of the Union

More Books for Writers:

www.authorlevelup.com/books

Fiction:

www.michaellaronn.com/books

93839132R00079